Amos

BRIDGE AT THE TOP

BRIDGE AT THE TOP

TERENCE REESE

with an Introduction by Victor Mollo

Faber and Faber · 3 Queen Square · London

00190

CONTENTS

Author's Foreword   *page* ix

Introduction by Victor Mollo   xi

1 Evidence of Promise   1

2 Juvenilia   6

3 The Big Match   12

4 Some Memorable Encounters   19

5 Bridge on the Air   27

6 Anti-Discovery   34

7 Trials—and Tribulations   40

8 The New Member   45

9 Two Auspicious Beginnings   52

10 A Slight Mystery   59

11 Not with Seemliness   67

12 Collision Course   74

13 A Big Build-up   80

14 A Strong Applaud   87

15 Traumatic End at Turin   96

16 Wind of Change   103

17 Little Major   110

18 Pug and the Stripe-tailed Ape   117

19 They Don't Grow on Trees   125

20 No Turkish Delight   132

. . . when all else fails—sport, love, ambition—bridge remains a solace and an entertainment.

Somerset Maugham in the British Bridge World

'You don't play whist, young man? You are laying up for yourself a dull old age.'

Ascribed to Talleyrand

AUTHOR'S FOREWORD

This book has four main strands: it is semi-autobiographical, describing my experiences in the game over a period of 50 years; it relates various happenings that are part of bridge history and might otherwise be forgotten; though not a textbook, it contains many hands chosen for their instructional value; and there are several stories, quotations and incidents that have amused me and will, I hope, amuse the reader.

One point I ought to mention is this: while I have written frankly, but I trust not unfairly, about people who are no longer with us, I have abstained from comparative comment about present-day players. Praise one, you antagonize another. What was that phrase of Ambrose Bierce? 'He is a person of low taste, more interested in himself than in me.'

The *Bridge Magazine, British Bridge World, Contract Bridge Journal* and American *Bridge World* have all assisted my recollection. When I have been unable to lay hands on a particular copy, G. C. H. Fox, of the Mayfair School of Bridge, or the firm of Bibliagora, has most kindly filled the gap.

TERENCE REESE

INTRODUCTION

by Victor Mollo

Terence Reese couldn't have chosen a better moment to come into the world. The good fairies who presided at his birth and dedicated the infant to bridge, so timed it that his life span should embrace every major event, from the dawn of Culbertson's golden era to the sad farewell of Italy's Blue Team at Monte Carlo.

As player, producer, writer, critic, in one capacity or another, Reese has always held the centre of the stage.

Turning over these pages, the reader will relive the history of bridge and meet its architects, and foremost among them Terence Reese himself, who cast so many of the spells that made the cauldron boil.

For a judgement of Reese as a player, I turn to this passage in the *Official Encyclopedia of Bridge*.

His numerous successes and infrequent failures in championships of every kind led him to be considered by many authorities the top-ranking player in the world.

On the technical plane there have been other virtuosos, but none since Culbertson have contributed so much to the game or exercised so profound an influence on modern thought. His masterly exposition of the theory of Restricted Choice in *The Expert Game* is an example that readily comes to mind.

Some men are born to greatness, others acquire it, but none at bridge have greatness thrust upon them. They must be born to it, then only can they rise to the top. And that is the story of Terence Reese.

A brilliant scholar, with talents in many directions, he could have made a name for himself in other walks of life. He preferred bridge. He came, he played, he conquered—and looking back on his life he has no regrets.

To reach the summit in any profession usually calls for single-minded concentration, the bending of all one's energies and gifts towards the desired goal. Terence never tried too hard. He didn't have to.

In the 40 years or more in which I've known him, he has always been deeply involved in every phase of bridge life, yet so far as I could see, he has never been under pressure.

Unlike other champions, he doesn't take his achievements too seriously. Perhaps he isn't fully conscious of them. It came to him as quite a surprise, when I asked him for bibliographic details, to discover that some 40 titles are listed under his name.

Books apart, he writes for two newspapers at home and for a host of magazines all over the world. He is also much in demand as commentator at International tournaments.

Terence admits that he is lazy. What would happen if he were not? It's an awesome thought.

Bridge at the Top is in no sense a textbook, yet the advanced player will learn more from it than from many an erudite treatise. For as he follows the author's experiences and his thought processes, he catches glimpses of how Reese himself evolved. He sees him pick up the threads in seemingly routine situations and come up, again and again, with new solutions to old problems.

You are East, defending a no trump contract, and at some stage you decide to switch to a suit in which dummy's holding is K 6. Which card do you lead from J 5 4 2?

The jack? Quite right, but how many players would think of it? Terence Reese tells you why it is the correct card to play—and how he came to discover it.

The book is studded with fascinating hands—hands that made history and hands that might well have done so had the setting been different. Reflections abound on theory, odds, percentages, psychology.

But these only provide the background for the story of Terence Reese, a story enlivened with anecdotes, enriched with human and humorous touches, and many a *bon mot* about the colourful and vibrant personalities in the world of bridge.

The caustic quip, the astringent comment, so characteristic of the earlier Reese, are still with us and always will be. But there's an unmistakable undertone of geniality which wasn't always there. Is that due to advancing years, established success, a happy marriage, or more likely, a combination of all three?

Whatever it is, there's something benign about Terence Reese these days, which didn't spring to the eyes before.

I notice it at the Eccentric Club whenever I table my hand to him as dummy. He still looks pained, of course, and winces occasionally, but he spares me the scathing remarks which run through his mind. He simply won't understand that being, unlike himself, a poor card holder, I can't afford to bid as soundly as he does.

I am always happy to cut Terence as my partner for he holds excellent cards—or maybe it's just the way he holds them.

Having read, re-read and edited this book, I expect that I shall hold mine better, too. But that's by the way. The purpose of *Bridge at the Top* is not to make people play better, but to present a personalized history of bridge in a way that hasn't been done before.

one

EVIDENCE OF PROMISE

Alas, I have the world's worst memory for day-to-day events and a conventional autobiography along the lines of 'my little sister, known to her friends as Podge' would be quite beyond me. But one recalls odd incidents, and reading old magazines stirs the memory cells. The reader must not expect an orderly narrative; the sequence is roughly chronological, but I may digress at any time.

My father was the youngest son of a Welsh clergyman. According to an aunt (who lived to the age of 100), the Reverend wanted me to inherit the collection of his sermons, but they were consumed in a bonfire before the week was out. Otherwise, how different . . .

My father began life in a Bank and transferred into the family catering business after marriage. Apart from his work, his life seemed to centre on his dogs and his motor-cars, but I remember, with a little sadness, my mother saying once, 'All he cares about in the world is you two boys.'

My mother came from a middle-class Victorian family. Her father owned a well-known chain of cafés and restaurants, with branches in several Surrey towns. I was born in a flat above the restaurant which still dominates Epsom High Street. My mother was clever at school and exceedingly capable in many fields. In addition, without being priggish, she had the disposition of an angel; I don't believe it was possible for a selfish thought to find its way into her mind.

With both parents in business, and an older brother, I was self-reliant, precocious and unsociable. At the age of five or six I used to travel on my own to kindergarten at Sutton, four miles away. I was supposed to be in the care of an older pupil on the train, but I used to avoid her. When my mother issued the standard warning about not talking to strange men, my father remarked that it was the strange men who should be warned against trying to talk to me.

My parents first met as 'First Gentleman' and 'First Lady' at a whist drive and I played card games before I could read. I had my first lessons in (Auction) bridge at the age of seven, when on holiday at Lulworth Cove, in Dorset. I used to dismount from my chair to sort my cards behind a cushion, 13 being somewhat of a handful. From then on we played fairly regularly *en famille*, father and brother making up with weary condescension against my mother and myself, the keen ones.

At my prep school, Bilton Grange, near Rugby, a very high-powered establishment, we played a sort of bridge occasionally, on Saturday evenings in the headmaster's study. At Bradfield I never saw a pack of cards, though I am sure there was no embargo on them. One day when I was home from school a game of bridge was organized and my respected parent opened 3 NT from hand. Such a call was non-existent at Auction and I was much annoyed at this display of adult frivolity.

'This is the bid that would be made at Contract', my mother told me. 'Mr Milton Work, an American writer, counts 4 points for an ace, 3 for a king, 2 for a queen, 1 for a jack. With 13 points you open 1 NT, with 17 2 NT, with 21 3 NT.'

I had nothing and we were two down. It was my first introduction to the point count and to contract bridge, and I was not impressed.

My mother was running a hotel, Merrow Grange, near Guildford, at this time, and as contract became popular a bridge club was soon formed. Thus I had a fair amount of practice and played in the earliest duplicate matches, round about 1930.

There was no organized bridge at Oxford, but there was a good player in my college, Charles McLaren, and with two friends of his we formed a team. In my last year, 1935, the Isis relayed a challenge issued in the Granta by one Iain Macleod. Charles took this up on our behalf and the *Bridge Magazine* offered to sponsor the match, which was to be played over 100 boards at the Albany Club in Savile Row. Some weeks before the contest, Charles took me to the club for a partnership. As we entered the cardroom he drew my attention to a bald-headed man with a small moustache and a high colour, smoking a pipe. 'That is the best player here', Charles said quietly. 'His name is Harrison-Gray.'

The match began in quite a tense atmosphere, before a gallery which included A. E. Manning-Foster, editor of *Bridge Magazine*, and Colonel Walter Buller. Colonel Buller (no publicity agent could have invented a better name) was the proponent of 'British Bridge' and the best-known figure in the game, as a result of his trenchant articles in the *Star* (a London evening paper). He was a violent critic of 'American Bridge' and the approach principle, recognized no forcing or artificial bids and contended that his direct method was the only honourable and efficient way of playing the game. In a famous match against the Culbertsons' his team was defeated, though not disgraced. Buller gave no ground, attributing the result to the failure of his team-mates (bewitched by American propaganda) to adhere to the purity of his principles.

It is because of Buller that I recall the first hand of the match. My partner and I held:

West	*East*
♠ x x	♠ A Q J x x
♡ J x	♡ A x x
◇ x	◇ A x x x
♣ A K Q 10 9 x x x	♣ x

Sitting West, I opened 5 ♣ and my partner gave me 6 ♣. A low spade was led, and when the dummy went down, with its three aces, I said, 'It's a pity you weren't playing with Colonel Buller, Charles: you could have bid 8 ♣.' Which raised quite a laugh.

I went up with ♠ A, of course, drew trumps, and gave up a spade, establishing a discard for my losing heart. As it turned out, the opening lead was a singleton and if I had finessed at trick 1, I would have lost the contract. My play was duly noted and considered as evidence of promise.

We won the match by about 4,000. Our second pair was stronger than theirs, who played with aristocratic languor but no great skill. Both the *Bridge Magazine* and the *British Bridge World* carried reports of the contest, muddling up the teams, misspelling the Colleges, and saying nothing of value.

When I came down from Oxford I worked for ten months at Harrods as a 'university trainee', but this wasn't likely to last and when Hubert Phillips asked me to do a regular job for the *British Bridge World*, of which he was editor, I accepted. I had already written my first book, *The Elements of Contract*, nominally in collaboration with him, breaking the back of it during a fortnight at Lynmouth, in North Devon, where my father had a restaurant and hotel business.

It was a part-time appointment, with the magnificent stipend of £2 a week. One of the differences between life then and now was that one didn't need much money and didn't bother about it, as one has to nowadays. After the evening game at Lederers, in Upper

Berkeley Street, we used to repair to the all-night restaurant at the Marble Arch Corner House, talk bridge and write hands on paper napkins until five in the morning. Porridge and cream 8*d*, coffee 1½*d*.

If you could knock up £250 a year one way or another, it was enough. Gray would only play 'for the house' at Lederers, which was not very remunerative. Nobody had a more cavalier attitude to money than his partner, S. J. Simon, author of *Why You Lose at Bridge* and other splendid books. With a total worldly capital of about 12/– he would descend to the street, call 'Cab', and proceed to the afternoon greyhound meeting at Stamford Bridge. On arrival, he would invest all that remained on some unlikely forecast, spurning the learned advices of *aficionados* such as Pedro Juan and myself. When the forecast went down he would approach some acquaintance at the track, hold out a grubby paw and say 'Give dollar'. With this he would charter another cab and return to the treadmill at the club, where he had a limited amount of credit.

Gray's other team-mates at this time were Iain Macleod and Jack Marx. Iain's transformation from a bridge layabout to Cabinet Minister, very nearly Prime Minister, was quite remarkable. I am surprised that Nigel Fisher did not make more of it in his book about Iain. He wrote to me, asking for my reminiscences of Macleod as a bridge player, and I told him some interesting things about Iain—factual, not unkind. He thanked me but included very little of this in his book; not wanting to rock the boat, I suppose.

The most brilliant of the young players at Lederers was 'Plum' Meredith, who spent the last part of his life in America and died early in 1976. He ran some little club in Wimbledon and at the conclusion of his labours used to drive to London in an extremely dusty, ramshackle car. He was known universally as 'Plum', but for 40 years, if he telephoned you, it was always 'Adam speaking' in a grave tone. Of course, one didn't know who it was from Adam.

I played part of my first season with Dick Lederer himself. He was a fine, instinctive, but also very experienced, player, and I learned a lot from him. In 1937 my mother started a new club in Guildford and I went back there for a time. She fell ill and died in 1939. When I returned to London, Lederers had moved from Upper Berkeley Street to less ambitious premises in the Bayswater Road. Dick was a big man in every way, but businesslike he was not. The new club was called the Tyburn. ('They used to hang criminals on this site', I remarked once after an 800 penalty. 'Pity they ever stopped.')

Early in the war a bomb dropped on the convent next door and I have a memory of poor Dick, who had a broken hip, sitting swathed in blankets on the pavement outside the club in the middle of the night. He died a year or two later. His wife, Peggy, kept the flag flying for several years in Mount Street, and his son, Tony, maintained the name at the Regency Club in Dorset Square. Apart from that, Dick is commemorated by the Richard Lederer Memorial Cup and, in another way, by the successes of British teams in the 1950s and 1960s, which consisted almost entirely of players who had developed their game under his friendly auspices.

two

JUVENILIA

My first appearance as a bridge journalist was in an article for the *British Bridge World* of March 1935, with the portentous title, 'The New Scoring: Its Effect on the Bidding'. In the previous code the penalties for vulnerable undertricks had been on the same scale as are now scored for doubled undertricks when not vulnerable; thus three down undoubled cost 500. I pointed out that with the revised scoring (such as we have now) trap passes lost some of their effect and psychic overcalls when vulnerable were less of a hazard than before. The article contained two hands, one of them a guard squeeze, though not so named. I do not have to blush for it.

My next contribution two months later was a different matter. It was called 'Are We Improved?' and was a review of the *Advanced Culbertson for 1935*. This recommended for the first time that a change of suit such as 1 ♠–2 ♡ should be forcing. As the opener was required to have a sound rebid, opening standards were raised. Imbued with the earliest Acol notions, I asked rhetorically whether opener was expected to pass on some rubbishy hands which I would not dream of opening today. Having examined the idea that a change of suit by responder should be forcing, I ended my review of the 'New Culbertson' with this egregious comment: 'But I do not believe that its principles either will be, or deserve to be, accepted by good players.'

In succeeding months I contributed a number of articles that were fairly advanced for the time and formed the basis of my later books on play. I also edited the monthly competition feature. Replying to a questionnaire, one reader described my competitions as a lottery, but another, a writer named Basset Scott, said that they 'helped those with brains to use them, and those without to realize the omission'; a remark I am vain enough to treasure.

Relations between the *British Bridge World* and the *Bridge Magazine* were not friendly. Manning-Foster had founded the *Bridge Magazine* in 1926 and the British Bridge League in 1931. He was a trim self-contained little man, a little like Clement Attlee in his bearing. After an accident in 1934 he always carried a stick. With columns in *The Times*, the *Observer* and the *Field*, he was the most successful professional in the game. He saw no reason why anyone should start a rival organization.

Hubert Phillips founded the *British Bridge World* in 1933 and the National Bridge Association at the same time. He was a cheerful, rotund, Pickwickian figure and a man of many parts. After the war he became nationally known for the omniscience he displayed in the radio programme, 'Round Britain Quiz'. His interest in bridge promotion arose from a friendship with Bernard Westall, chairman of De La Rue. Cards were something of a blind spot for him, but he brought enormous zest to the game and a succession of astonishing puns that kept everyone in fits of laughter. (Once at an Irish Congress he played in a team with Yorkshireman, Ben Cohen. Ben opened light and became increasingly alarmed as Hubert carried the bidding to a high level. When Hubert put down a wonderful dummy his partner's face lightened. 'What they call *Ben Trovato*',* said Hubert.)

In all his writings Manning-Foster adopted a benign, patriarchal pose, addressing himself to 'amateur' and family players. His attitude to tournament bridge was somewhat ambivalent. At a time when he was President of both the British Bridge League and the International Bridge League he expressly approved the sentiments (though not, I dare say, the literary form) of this paragraph by Dr Melville Smith in the *Evening News*:

Unlike cricket, the great majority of Bridge players don't care a hang about the big matches, nor are they in the slightest degree interested in the prowess of the 'champions' or their systems; they don't even know their names.

Nor would they have learned them from *Bridge Magazine*, which contained some cosy reading but seldom anything of interest to a serious player. There were endless diatribes against conventions, the editor waffled away on his 'Simple System of Bidding' and a number of military gentlemen contributed their recollections. Of the regular features, the one that we awaited each month with joyful expectation was 'Leaves from a Bridge Player's Diary' by one H. L. Thorneley. This excerpt will give an idea of his breathless style and notions of the game:

---

* 'Well found' in Italian; thus extremely apt.

13th July

Contract at K's. All square on four rubbers. This is the tale of a game handed to me on a silver platter when these were the cards:

```
                    ♠ K 8 4
                    ♡ A J
                    ◇ 10 9 7 5 3 2
                    ♣ A Q
      ♠ A Q 9 3 2                  ♠ J 10 6
      ♡ 9 8 7 5         Y          ♡ K 6
      ◇ 6           A       B      ◇ K Q J 4
      ♣ 4 3 2           Z          ♣ 10 9 7 5
                    ♠ 7 5
                    ♡ Q 10 4 3 2
                    ◇ A 8
                    ♣ K J 8 6
```

As Z, vulnerable at a love score, I called 'One Heart', a bid based on the Losing Trick Count—more of this anon—A passed, Y made it 'Two Diamonds', B passed, I switched to 'Two No Trumps', Y raised to 'Three' and the Three of Spades was the opening lead.

In the play A led a low spade, B held the first trick with the 10 and switched to ◇ K. Some declarers might grab this and play on hearts, but our hero ducks and B determinedly follows with ◇ Q. Z now gets the diamonds going and makes his contract. 'Good old Losing Trick Count' is the conclusion, with no animadversion upon the play of ◇ Q.

One of my earliest contributions to the *British Bridge World* was a skit on this, entitled 'Sheaves from a Bridge Player's Library', by A. Rose Without. (*A Rose Without a Thorn* was a celebrated play at the time.) It began as follows:

2nd February

Contract at K's. Played five rubbers, lost six. I had an exasperating experience on this hand:

```
                         ♠ 7 6 3
                         ♡ 10 5 4 3 2
                         ◇ J 10 8 4 2
                         ♣ None
   ♠ None                               ♠ 8 5 4 2
   ♡ None               Y               ♡ 9 8 7 6
   ◇ None           A       B           ◇ 9 7 6 5 3
   ♣ A K Q J 10 9 8 7 6 5 4 3 2         ♣ None
                         Z
                         ♠ A K Q J 10 9
                         ♡ A K Q J
                         ◇ A K Q
                         ♣ None
```

I was Z and at a love score A dealt and bid 'Seven Clubs'. Y passed, with my galaxy of Aces and Kings I naturally doubled, A redoubled, Y passed, B hesitated for a long while but finally passed, and I passed. Four of Diamonds was Y's lead, I played Ace, A trumped and led Ace of Clubs. When both Y and B discarded on this trick I quickly realized I might be in difficulties later on and set myself to watch Y's discards like a hawk. Sure enough, by the eleventh trick I had two Aces and the King of Diamonds left. A ran another Club, I threw the Ace of Spades, yet another Club followed and I was squeezed. After a lot of thought I threw Ace of Hearts and now the critical moment had arrived. Judge my consternation when A produced the Two of Clubs for thirteenth trick and contract!

Y pointed out that A could have exposed his hand earlier and saved us the worry of discarding. I agreed, but A said he enjoyed watching us struggle when all along he felt almost sure to make his contract. Well, it all depends on the point of view, and certainly I would not wish to spoil A's pleasures.

Another ridiculous hand followed, and the piece ended with a line suggested by Skid (S. J. Simon):

20th February

Contract at K's. Not invited. Curious.

The British Bridge League and the National Bridge Association carried out independent programmes, in competition with one another. The *Bridge Magazine* never mentioned N.B.A. events. In 1936 Hubert carried the battle into the international field by forming the Duplicate Bridge Board of Control. This body, which had the backing on paper of almost all the leading figures of the day, coolly assumed control of practically everything in the tournament field, including the selection of international teams. The B.B.L. was invited to contribute three delegates. At the same time the London and Home Counties Contract Bridge Association and, shortly afterwards, the English Bridge Union were established as makeweights.

Hubert's justification for usurping the powers the B.B.L. had previously enjoyed was that the League had always been a completely autocratic body. In theory, its decisions were made by its Council, which in turn was composed of local secretaries; but as these were appointed by Manning-Foster himself, the League's governing body was simply an extension of his own authority. 'There has been a strong reaction against organization from the top and a demand for organization from the bottom', Hubert declared.

Bridge players were not interested in political formulae, but they were (as always) dissatisfied with methods of team selection. Britain had never finished in the first three in the International Bridge League's tournaments; not surprisingly, perhaps, for according to Harry Ingram (a leading international at the time) the President's regular injunction to the players was not to worry about winning or losing, so long as they upheld the traditions of British sportsmanship.

The B.B.L., predictably, ignored the D.B.B.C. and the next development was a Players' Manifesto. In January 1937 Hubert was writing:

> The manifesto of a number of leading players—including, I understand, Lederer, Konstam, Mathieson, Gray, Kempson and Simon—is a significant assertion of democratic control. These players have refused to allow their names to be considered for a team that claims to be nationally representative unless the properly constituted authority—the Duplicate Bridge Board of Control—endorses, or is responsible for, its selection.

The B.B.L. made its plans for the European Championship at Budapest with such resources as remained. The phalanx of the Players' Manifesto did not remain unbroken for long. Konstam and Mathieson, ceasing to assert democratic control, were there when the tapes went up. The team was completed by two B.B.L. loyalists from Birmingham, Reeve and Lock, who had won the National Pairs but were no great shakes. They finished fifth out of seven at Budapest.

The following year the B.B.L. committed itself to sending the Gold Cup winners to The Hague. This worked out quite well, Dodds-Bach, Tottenham-Cotter finishing second to Hungary. The Duplicate Bridge Board of Control, blocked on the international front, found justification for its existence in the activities of the English, Scottish, Welsh and two Irish Unions. It was not revived after the war.

There was rivalry in those days between different groups of players, as well as between the controlling bodies. A match in the semi-final of the 1937 Gold Cup, played at the Bexhill Congress, was considered to be a particularly significant encounter. On one side was Gray's team, all from Lederers and pioneers of Acol; on the other, Mathieson, Konstam, Dodds, Summers, Simmons, players with more experience and, in their own opinion, more natural talent. After an even first half Gray won by a fair margin. Konstam wrote a celebrated 'open letter' to the *British Bridge World* in which he congratulated Gray on his victory but went on to imply that his team lacked the necessary flair to achieve success at international level. 'You started life with four sound players. But you were handicapped. You had no Buller, no Kehoe, no Lederer as inspiration . . . I should be far more impressed if I could point to any one piece of brilliance, any one bid that lifted the side out of "perfect" mediocrity . . . You mapped out for yourselves an inexorable par below which nothing can induce you to fall, but above which (I know you will forgive the liberty) you seem unable to rise.'

In reply, Iain Macleod wrote a piece in the style of the Western Brothers, cabaret entertainers who wore white tie and tails and sang songs at the piano with exaggerated old-boy accents. These were the first three verses:

The 'K.K.' System or 'Rising Above Par'

We lost a match at Bexhill—biggest shock we've ever had:
And how we lost I still can't think, the whole thing's rather sad,
For Gray is mediocre and the rest are frankly bad,
    Only par, chaps, only par!

We overbid on every hand and never cared a damn,
We think it's better to go down for mutton than for lamb;
We always think a one-bid should be forcing to a slam,
    Beating par, chaps, beating par!

You should never stop in part-scores, for that is far too tame,
And once in every hundred boards you'll find you've missed a game;
And if we haven't got a bid we open just the same,
    Beating par, chaps, beating par!

Good enough, in my opinion, to suggest that Iain could have made a name for himself in other fields than bridge and politics.

three

THE BIG MATCH

From 1929 to 1939 was an era of big challenge matches. In this chapter I write about the most famous of all, the Culbertson-Lenz 'Bridge Battle of the Century' in 1931. I was not present, of course, but I feel that I 'know' it from the marvellous book on the match in which hands were analysed from three angles—by 'Mr Culbertson and his partners', by Jacoby, and by the referee, Lt (later General) Gruenther.

Culbertson's *Blue Book*, published in 1930, and the Summary that followed it, had enormous sales and placed him far ahead of his rivals. The opposition gathered under the banner of the Official 1-2-3 System. This was not a natural system on Buller lines, but opening bids of two were strong and bids of three were forcing. By far its most famous exponent was Sidney Lenz, author of *Lenz on Bridge* and *More Lenz on Bridge*, which both in a technical and a literary sense were the best books ever written on Auction. Lenz chose as his partner Oswald Jacoby, who was not a member of the Official group but who remained in the front rank of American bridge for very many years.

The terms of the contest were that it should consist of 150 rubbers, that Culbertson should play at least half the time with his wife, and that Lenz and his partner should adhere to the Official method. Culbertson, who owed nothing to Mohammed Ali in pre-match publicity, laid his opponent 5,000 dollars to 1,000 dollars, the winnings to go to charity.

The match was played in a glare of publicity such as has never attended any other bridge game nor ever will again. The day-by-day scores were front-page news in 30 countries and every move was reported on the radio.

Lenz and Jacoby were the first to strike the front. One of their good hands was interesting in both a historical and technical sense.

East dealer
Love all

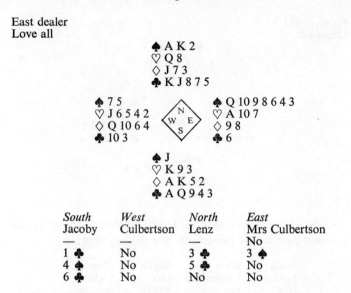

```
              ♠ A K 2
              ♡ Q 8
              ◇ J 7 3
              ♣ K J 8 7 5

♠ 7 5                          ♠ Q 10 9 8 6 4 3
♡ J 6 5 4 2         N          ♡ A 10 7
◇ Q 10 6 4     W       E       ◇ 9 8
♣ 10 3             S           ♣ 6

              ♠ J
              ♡ K 9 3
              ◇ A K 5 2
              ♣ A Q 9 4 3
```

South	West	North	East
Jacoby	Culbertson	Lenz	Mrs Culbertson
—	—	—	No
1 ♣	No	3 ♣	3 ♠
4 ♠	No	5 ♣	No
6 ♣	No	No	No

Jacoby says in his commentary that after his partner's jump raise—
obviously a big bid in the system—he had decided to go for a slam
in any case and had bid 4 ♠ in the hope of averting a spade lead.
Whether he would have been successful in this objective will never
be known, for Mrs Culbertson led ♡ A out of turn. In those days
you could call for a lead when that happened. Jacoby requested a
diamond lead and had no problems when dummy's jack held the
first trick.

It was assumed at the time that a spade or club lead would have
broken the contract, but from juvenile scribblings made 45 years ago
I see that I noted a way to make it. Suppose that a spade is led.
Declarer wins, draws trumps and leads a low heart from the table.
When the king wins (it does not help East to go up with the ace)
South throws a heart on the second spade, ruffs a spade, cashes
◇ A K and exits with a heart. Then East is forced to concede a ruff-
and-discard.

Lenz and Jacoby held the lead for 43 rubbers, but then a steep
decline set in, which culminated in Jacoby's resignation after the
103rd rubber. Three hands, in particular, led to this event. The first
was described at the time as the greatest tragedy of the match:

South dealer
Game all

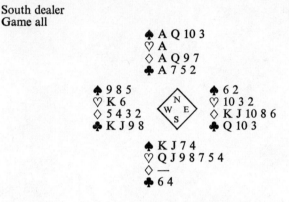

```
              ♠ A Q 10 3
              ♡ A
              ◇ A Q 9 7
              ♣ A 7 5 2
  ♠ 9 8 5                      ♠ 6 2
  ♡ K 6          N             ♡ 10 3 2
  ◇ 5 4 3 2   W     E          ◇ K J 10 8 6
  ♣ K J 9 8      S             ♣ Q 10 3
              ♠ K J 7 4
              ♡ Q J 9 8 7 5 4
              ◇ —
              ♣ 6 4
```

Culbertson was playing with Teddy Lightner, founder of the Lightner slam double convention. The bidding went:

South Jacoby	West Culbertson	North Lenz	East Lightner
1 ♡	No	3 NT	No
4 ♡	No	4 NT	No
5 ♡	No	6 NT	No
No	Dble	No	No
7 ♡	Dble	No	No
No			

Lenz's devotion to no trumps and the four aces was ascribed to his Auction upbringing. Still, with his two A-Qs I don't think his 6 NT was unreasonable. Jacoby, having issued two warnings, might have let him take his chance in this contract. Culbertson warmly congratulated himself on his brilliant psychology in doubling 6 NT, which is cold except against a club lead.

The next critical moment occurred in the 97th rubber.

South dealer
Game all, E-W 35

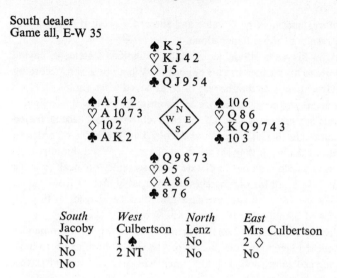

♠ K 5
♡ K J 4 2
◇ J 5
♣ Q J 9 5 4

♠ A J 4 2
♡ A 10 7 3
◇ 10 2
♣ A K 2

♠ 10 6
♡ Q 8 6
◇ K Q 9 7 4 3
♣ 10 3

♠ Q 9 8 7 3
♡ 9 5
◇ A 8 6
♣ 8 7 6

South	West	North	East
Jacoby	Culbertson	Lenz	Mrs Culbertson
No	1 ♠	No	2 ◇
No	2 NT	No	No
No			

As the first trick in no trumps counted 35, and East-West had 35 below, this was a game bid. Lenz led ♣ Q, on which Jacoby played the 7 and Culbertson held off. Lenz continued with ♣ J and now Jacoby dropped the 8. West won and led ◇ 10 to the king, which held; returning to ♡ A, he led another diamond, which South won.

Realizing that three clubs, a diamond and ♡ K would not be enough to beat the contract, Jacoby did not clear the clubs but switched to ♠ 3. This was high-class play, but the fall of the clubs had been confusing and when Lenz came in with ♠ K he returned a spade instead of clearing the clubs. From his angle, it looked as though West's remaining clubs were K 6. After the hand, Lenz started the offensive and his criticisms were not well received, Jacoby observing that he had made a play that only twelve experts in the country would understand, and unfortunately Mr Lenz did not appear, at that particular moment, to be one of them.

The deal that led to the final argument was not particularly interesting. Jacoby, as quite often, bid away on nothing. His antics had no bearing on the result, but Lenz was indignant. 'What do you mean by bidding on absolutely nothing? You are just having a lot of fun bidding as you do, and I am always in the dark as to what you actually mean. Give me a break once in while.' Jacoby's psychic ventures had great news value and showed a profit if one analyses the results of those hands alone.

After his resignation Jacoby made a dignified statement, paying tribute to his partner and his opponents. What upset him, according to Gruenther, was that he was often attacked when (in his opinion) it was his partner who had made the mistake. I know the feeling.

It is not surprising that the nerves of all the players became frayed at times. Both Culbertson and Jacoby had the habit of ordering large steaks when they sat down at the table. When dummy, Culbertson would rush out to dictate to his secretary or speak over the radio. As in all his big matches, he invariably arrived from one to two hours late. On the one occasion when he arrived on time he observed blandly that his watch was wrong.

Jacoby's place as Lenz's partner was taken by Commander Winfield Liggett, Jr. 'Lig', as his partner called him, seems to have performed quite well, but not much was heard of him after this match.

During the sixteenth session the Culbertson lead reached its highest point, 20,535. It escaped Ely's notice that he could have been defeated on the following hand:

East dealer
Love all

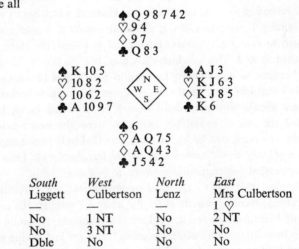

```
                    ♠ Q 9 8 7 4 2
                    ♡ 9 4
                    ◇ 9 7
                    ♣ Q 8 3
    ♠ K 10 5                        ♠ A J 3
    ♡ 10 8 2          N             ♡ K J 6 3
    ◇ 10 6 2      W       E         ◇ K J 8 5
    ♣ A 10 9 7        S             ♣ K 6
                    ♠ 6
                    ♡ A Q 7 5
                    ◇ A Q 4 3
                    ♣ J 5 4 2
```

South	West	North	East
Liggett	Culbertson	Lenz	Mrs Culbertson
—	—	—	1 ♡
No	1 NT	No	2 NT
No	3 NT	No	No
Dble	No	No	No

North's lead of a spade is evidence that lead-directing doubles were not yet in vogue. Declarer won the first trick with ♠ 10 and led a diamond, the jack losing to the queen. Liggett returned a low club, covered by the 10, queen and king. A diamond from dummy was passed by South and won by the 10. Culbertson then switched to hearts and established two tricks in this suit before the defence could arrive at a trick in clubs.

Culbertson's account of the deal was headed 'A Fine Rebid to Game'. As to the play, he suggested that South would have done better to take ◇ A on the second round of the suit and continue clubs before the hearts had been developed. He noted, however, that the contract could still have been made by a throw-in.

The interesting point about the hand is that when South led clubs at trick 2 the right card was the jack, not the low one. This type of play tends to be right also when a defender holds Q x x x or J x x x, can see A 10 x x on his left and suspects K x on his right.

After a break for Christmas, during which Culbertson took the occasion to send his opponents an autographed copy of the new *Blue Book*, the match was resumed in January and the Culbertson lead began to dwindle. During this period he played one session with Mike Gottlieb and one with Howard Schenken, who were later to become a famous partnership in the Four Aces team. Josephine returned for the final session, which was fairly level, the final margin being 8,980. On the last hand of the match the Culbertsons played in five diamonds and made six owing to a lucky lie of the cards. In his radio speech, an hour after the match, Lenz referred to this deal. He got the details of the bidding and result a bit mixed up, but the thought was there: 'They bid 6 ◇, and they made 5 ◇', he said. 'Long live the Approach Forcing System!'

The Official system did not survive the match. Lenz himself was faithful to the intermediate two-bid but did not seem to know how to follow it up. His partners often failed to open the two-bid when they had the material for it, causing Ely to claim a foul. Lenz retired from tournament bridge after this contest but never lost his high esteem among American players. When we played the world championship match in New York in 1955 we were all very proud that he—and Jo Culbertson also—came more than once to watch the play.

I met Culbertson a few times on public occasions but only once in private conversation. It was in about 1949 and by this time I had begun to acquire what juvenile delinquents called a 'rep'. Ely phoned me out of the blue, having been given my number by Hubert Phillips. He said he was most interested in my career, wanted to discuss various projects, would I meet him for lunch at Ciro's? At the lunch my career was not mentioned; Culbertson talked only about his pre-eminent position in the States, the jealousy and ineffectuality of his rivals. I dare say I had this occasion in mind when after his death in 1955 I wrote:

The truth is that, like the dictators, though in a less sinister way, Ely was the victim of his own propaganda. Meeting him, one waited for the give-away line, the deprecatory remark to show that all the ballyhoo was—well, ballyhoo. It never came.

Looking back, I can see that I didn't know him well enough to make such a judgement. That remark about his watch being wrong was tremendous.

A passage in a recent article causes me to add a postscript to this chapter. Describing 'Early Days' for *Bridge Magazine*, George F. Hervey wrote:

Culbertson was no great bridge player. His best friends rated him no better than of average club standard, and some of us thought he was not as good as that. His success was due to the fact that he was a master of publicity. His wife, Josephine, was an excellent player and teacher.

The great French player, Pierre Albarran, expressed a different view in the course of a tribute to Culbertson in *Le Bridge*. This (in translation) is what he said:

I take this opportunity to destroy a legend that has spread among bridge players all over the world. With an air of being in the know, people have implied that Culbertson, while an excellent business-man, was only a moderate bridge player, much inferior to his wife. Josephine was an excellent player, to be sure, who made very few mistakes, but let us go no further. Ely, on the other hand, was a player of genius, liable to an occasional black-out, it is true, but of an originality in attack such as has not been surpassed by any player in the world, even by the greatest champions of today.

four

SOME MEMORABLE ENCOUNTERS

There were some big international clashes in Britain during the 1930s. First was the Buller-Culbertson match, then the two Schwab Cup matches in 1933 and 1934. The donor, Charles M. Schwab, was a steel magnate; what became of his trophy is obscure.

Culbertson's opponents in 1933 were Colonel Beasley and Sir Guy Domville, George Morris and Percy Tabbush. Beasley was correspondent on the *Daily Mail* at the time. Guy, handsome and debonair, was a popular figure in the London clubs for many years. George Morris was a famous gambler at every card game and also an athlete; he made a Channel-swimming attempt and played marathon golf for big stakes. His health failed and he was a pitiable figure in his later years. Tabbush followed a course that is not common among bridge players: he joined a religious sect and turned his back on the 'Devil's playthings'.

The match was played at Selfridges and was presented to an audience on a display board, the forerunner of bridgerama. Harold Thorne, author of the immensely successful *Contract Bridge in 20 Minutes*, was in charge of the board. Thorne was an inventor by profession; he had met Ely when travelling by ship to England three years before and had obtained permission to do a potted version of the *Blue Book*. He did not play bridge *at all*; it makes one think.

In addition to the demonstration board, there were glass spy-holes through which it was possible to watch the players. As my mother was performing some official duty, I managed to gain entry to the playing room itself during the first session. An evening news-paper, I remember, had a banner headline across the back page: CULBERTSON COMPLAINS OF BOARDS CARDS CHAIRS. All that had happened was that Ely had pointed out that the cards did not fit the duplicate boards, nor, obviously, the boards the cards; and he had requested a hard-backed chair for his wife. It hardly seemed necessary to have a back to her chair at all, for she sat upright, like a teacher of deportment.

The Americans won fairly comfortably against a team that lacked experience in systemic bidding. The match the following year was a different matter: this time the opposition consisted of two very

B

experienced partnerships, Lederer and Rose, Ingram and Hughes. The match was played at the Dorchester over five days, with two sessions of 30 boards a day.

The British soon went ahead, building up a lead of over 5,000 in the first three days. The Americans had not met a player like Dick Lederer, who took the shortest route to game, and Ingram and Hughes were always capable of imaginative strokes. Mrs Culbertson and Albert Morehead, on the other hand, seemed to be frozen by the dictates of the System. Guess their final contract on these two hands:

South	North
♠ 10 2	♠ A J 9
♡ 8	♡ K J 10
◇ A K J 10 8 4 3	◇ Q 7 2
♣ K 4 2	♣ Q J 7 5

You won't guess: they threw it in! South had a 'second-round' bid, while North lacked the statutory 2½ quick tricks. On another occasion Mrs Culbertson opened 1 ♡ on ♠ Q ♡ A K Q J 5 2 ◇ A K Q 4 ♣ J 6, as she lacked the 5 quick tricks for a two-bid. She played there, with 6 ◇ on, as partner held ♣ A and four diamonds.

On Wednesday, the third day, Ingram and Hughes took the evening off. It was a tiring match, and these two were going to their offices every morning. The reserve pair, Colonel Walshe and Kenneth Frost, held the fort successfully, dropping only a few points. In the afternoon session on Thursday the lead climbed to 5,000 again, and during the tea interval Ingram suggested to Dick that he and Willie Rose should rest for the evening session and be fresh for the last day. Dick did not fancy the idea, said Ingram darkly. From this moment a collapse set in. The home team dropped 3,000 in the remainder of the afternoon and a further 3,000 in the evening, to finish the day 990 behind.

The score fluctuated on the Friday afternoon, and when the last session began the Americans led by 970. In this tense situation the most publicized deal of the match occurred:

North dealer
Love all

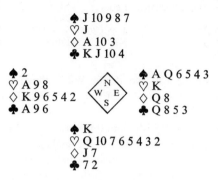

```
                    ♠ J 10 9 8 7
                    ♡ J
                    ◇ A 10 3
                    ♣ K J 10 4
    ♠ 2                              ♠ A Q 6 5 4 3
    ♡ A 9 8           N             ♡ K
    ◇ K 9 6 5 4 2   W   E           ◇ Q 8
    ♣ A 9 6           S             ♣ Q 8 5 3
                    ♠ K
                    ♡ Q 10 7 6 5 4 3 2
                    ◇ J 7
                    ♣ 7 2
```

This was the bidding in Room 1:

South	West	North	East
Ingram	Culbertson	Hughes	Lightner
—	—	1 ♠	No
No	Dble	No	No
1 NT	Dble	No	No
2 ◇	Dble	No	No
2 ♡	Dble	No	No
No			

As Ingram and Hughes played a 1 ♣ system, Ingram could afford to pass the opening 1 ♠. When West doubled and East passed, he employed diversionary tactics, hoping to be doubled in hearts at a low level. It is admitted that when 2 ◇ was doubled he hesitated for a few moments, as he was wondering whether to bid a deceptive 2 ♠.

West led a spade to the ace against 2 ♡ doubled and a low spade was returned. Instead of discarding his diamond loser, Ingram had a black-out and ruffed. West overruffed and the contract went one down.

Culbertson should have been happy to gain a plus score on the deal, but he was furious and rounded first on Hughes, asking why he had passed 2 ♡ with a singleton. 'My partner passed 1 ♠ and has been doubled in 2 ◇. I am sure he doesn't want to be put into three,' Stan told him, with some point. Then Ely turned on Ingram: 'How dare you hesitate after being doubled in 2 ◇?' He calmed down eventually. But if the contract had been made . . .?

The bidding at the other table was utterly horrendous:

South	*West*	*North*	*East*
Mrs Culbertson	Lederer	Morehead	Rose
—	—	No	No
3 ♡	4 ◇ (??)	4 ♠ (???)	5 ◇ (???)
No	No	Dble	No
No	No		

This was three down. No doubt Willie thought the 4 ♠ call was a bluff on the way to 5 ♡. Even so, there could be no harm in doubling it.

In the run-in the British team threw away 2,000 points in a desperate attempt to turn the tide, and the final margin was 3,650 to the Culbertsons. One is bound to wonder whether, with a strong captain, the home players might have held their early lead.

In the following year, 1935, Gottlieb and Schenken, now a partnership in the Four Aces team, came to England to play a challenge match of 100 rubbers against Ingram and Hughes. The Americans, no doubt, were a good deal stronger than any pair in the Culbertson team, while Ingram and Hughes played below form after a discouraging start. The visitors won by 7,000 odd. The match created great interest and it was not easy to obtain a seat in the small stand at the Dorchester. The session I watched contained a classic example of the Scissors Coup, known then as the Coup Without a Name. Ingram at the time was playing with his stand-by partner, Herbert Newmark.

East dealer
N-S vulnerable

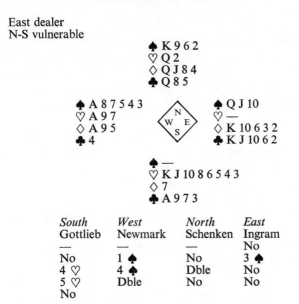

♠ K 9 6 2
♡ Q 2
◇ Q J 8 4
♣ Q 8 5

♠ A 8 7 5 4 3   ♠ Q J 10
♡ A 9 7   ♡ —
◇ A 9 5   ◇ K 10 6 3 2
♣ 4   ♣ K J 10 6 2

♠ —
♡ K J 10 8 6 5 4 3
◇ 7
♣ A 9 7 3

South	West	North	East
Gottlieb	Newmark	Schenken	Ingram
—	—	—	No
No	1 ♠	No	3 ♠
4 ♡	4 ♣	Dble	No
5 ♡	Dble	No	No
No			

West led his singleton club to the 10 and ace. Declarer played a heart
to the queen and returned a heart to the jack and ace. Newmark now
underled ◇ A; Ingram returned a *low* club for his partner to ruff, and
declarer still had two more clubs to lose. This excellent defence
brought in a penalty of 800. Gottlieb had a chance to save a trick,
however; when in dummy with ♡ Q he could have led ♠ K from
the table, discarding his singleton diamond. Then the ruff is averted
and South makes a second club trick by force.

The American pair played some other, less publicized, matches
against English pairs, winning them all quite easily. Later in the
year the Four Aces played a match against France, the European
champions, in New York. It was an ambitious affair, the last
session being staged at Madison Square Gardens, with live per-
formers representing the 52 cards. But as Schenken wryly remarks
in his book, *The Education of a Bridge Player*, interest flagged when
the home team, behind at first, went into the lead. The big final
night was a success as a spectacle, a failure as a promotion.

Two years later there was another memorable encounter when Dr

Paul Stern, responding to a private invitation, brought his famous Austrian team to England. They were European champions and had beaten the Culbertsons as well. The team included Schneider and Jellinek, a pair with a legendary reputation. The home team was an uneasy amalgam of players from three different groups: Konstam and Mathieson, Gray and Merkin, with Ewart Kempson as fifth man.

I saw a good deal of the play and it has always been a bit of a mystery to me why the Austrians won so easily (10,910 points over 300 boards). None of the home team played badly and the Austrian bidding certainly gave them chances.

The match had some stormy moments. At one point Jellinek opened 1 ♣, conventional but not strong in the Austrian system, and Mathieson made a trap pass on a good hand. However, Schneider on this occasion passed 1 ♣; it went four down, but the English pair had missed an easy game. According to Gray in the *British Bridge World*, 'The free-for-all that followed was mildly disconcerting, players, non-playing captains, officials and spectators joining in the argument till the roof of the Waldorf threatened to fall in'. Konstam's version was: 'We made a protest and accepted the referee's decision without more ado.'

Gray concluded his article with some observations not calculated to endear him to his team-mates. 'At the end of every 16 hands a pantomime took place for the benefit of the spectators, Konstam and Mathieson affirming that they had just done "better than par", while in view of the mounting deficit Merkin and myself felt compelled to assume a touching expression of guilt.' I doubt whether that comment gave an altogether fair impression; in my experience, Konstam was always a most agreeable team-mate.

The most publicized hands from the match were two slam deals where Jellinek went down in contracts which, on a strict analysis, he might have made. I found this deal entertaining:

North dealer
Game all

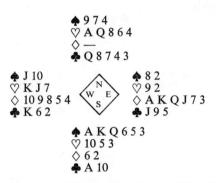

```
                    ♠ 9 7 4
                    ♡ A Q 8 6 4
                    ◇ —
                    ♣ Q 8 7 4 3
    ♠ J 10                         ♠ 8 2
    ♡ K J 7                        ♡ 9 2
    ◇ 10 9 8 5 4                   ◇ A K Q J 7 3
    ♣ K 6 2                        ♣ J 9 5
                    ♠ A K Q 6 5 3
                    ♡ 10 5 3
                    ◇ 6 2
                    ♣ A 10
```

Already, it would seem, a follower of the Losing Trick Count, Gray opened the bidding as North and made a slam try later.

South	West	North	East
Merkin	Herbert	Gray	Bludhorn
—	—	1 ♡	2 ◇
3 ♠	4 ◇	No	No
4 ♠	No	5 ◇ (!)	No
5 ♠	No	No	No

Herbert led a low club to the jack and ace. With the cards lying well, Merkin made twelve tricks.

The English pair were probably content with their score of 680, but there was bad news to come from the other table.

South	West	North	East
Schneider	Konstam	Jellinek	Mathieson
—	—	No	1 ◇
2 ♣ (!)	2 NT	3 ♣	3 NT
Dble	No	No	No

Schneider's overcall of two clubs, diverting attention from the suit where the real danger lay, was a type of psychic not uncommon in Auction days. Here the cards combined in a devilish way to assist him, both East and West pushing forward on the strength of the same feature. A club was led and the defence took the first nine tricks, for a penalty of 1,400.

On the last day of the match Konstam played with Merkin and Mathieson played 'British Bridge' with Kempson. On the Austrian side, Paul Stern played a few boards with Schneider. This was one of them:

North dealer
N-S vulnerable

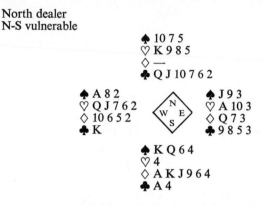

                    ♠ 10 7 5
                    ♡ K 9 8 5
                    ◇ —
                    ♣ Q J 10 7 6 2

    ♠ A 8 2   ♠ J 9 3
    ♡ Q J 7 6 2   ♡ A 10 3
    ◇ 10 6 5 2   ◇ Q 7 3
    ♣ K   ♣ 9 8 5 3

                    ♠ K Q 6 4
                    ♡ 4
                    ◇ A K J 9 6 4
                    ♣ A 4

Schneider played as South in 3 ◇. Konstam led ♡ Q and switched
to ♠ A, which created no problem. A switch to ♣ K at trick 2, not
easy to find, especially if you place declarer with the ace, beats the
contract, because a club ruff comes later and West can exit with a
heart.

At the other table, after two passes, Kempson opened 3 ◇, a
strong bid in his 'direct' system. Mathieson converted to 3 NT. East
led ♣ 9 and the singleton king fell under the ace at trick 1.

For 20 years, on and off, Kempson and I exchanged banter
about his bidding methods for the amusement of our readers, and
there was an opportunity here. 'At the conclusion of the informative
exchanges in Room 2', I wrote with ponderous irony, 'North was in
a makable contract after the fall of ♣ K on the first trick.' Mathieson must have miscounted his tricks, for instead of knocking out
♠ A at trick 2 he played off the ace and king of diamonds, setting
up a fifth winner for the defence.

Stanley Merkin, who had a good match in difficult circumstances,
always preferred watching to playing. He is known in the London
clubs as the Senior Kibitzer, entertaining us from time to time with
flashes of bucolic humour. Once in the canasta days a Mrs Oppen-
heimer, Miss Inskipp and Mrs James came into the card room at
Crockford's together. 'Here come Hoppy, Skippy and Jumpy',
Stanley announced.

five

BRIDGE ON THE AIR

Some months before war broke out I made a shrewd safety play by joining the A.R.P. (Air Raid Precautions). When I was due for call-up the blitz was at its height and I was told that my call-up would be deferred during the emergency. By accident or design, the military made no further attempt to coerce me. The Ministry of Labour sought me out, however, and there was a ludicrous period in which I was assigned to work in a factory which manufactured lamp brackets, or gas brackets, whatever they were. My old friend, Pedro Juan, was much amused by the injunction of a foreman who, seeing me engaged in some constructional task, called out, 'Don't 'urt the 'ammer, mate!'

Later on I was enrolled in Pedro's own firm, which made black-out curtains. Once an inspector from the Ministry of Labour called, to see whether I was performing my duties. 'Our Mr Reese is at the other factory, about a mile from here', Pedro told him. By the time the man from the Ministry got there on his flat feet, there I was, surrounded by various important-looking ledgers.

Skid (S. J. Simon) was a warden on the same post in Cumberland Place. One night there was an 'incident' on the outskirts of our territory which called for the urgent summoning of help, fire-fighting equipment and so forth. Skid and I set off for our head-quarters at his usual three-mile-an-hour shuffle, the object of our mission soon forgotten in the course of some theoretical discussion. When we were about 20 yards from the post Skid came to a halt, then said, 'Suggest quick walk. To arrive panting.'

The London Association organized one or two wartime events, but there was nothing on a national scale. When the war in Europe ended and the national bodies made no move to reconstitute themselves, I took the initiative in forming the Tournament Bridge Association. I had excellent support from everyone who counted in the bridge world at the time and my partner in the enterprise, a poker-playing friend from Crockford's named Harold Selby, was by profession an advertising and promotion man.

Towards the end of 1946 the B.B.L. and the E.B.U., now part of the same set-up, slowly heaved themselves to their feet. It was put

to me by intermediaries that the T.B.A. should disband itself, but
neither our Executive Committee nor players at large wanted this,
for it was not disputed that the T.B.A. had set new standards in
tournament promotion. A period of uneasy conflict followed.
Manning-Foster had died in 1939 and the new President of the
B.B.L., Noel Mobbs (later Sir Noel Mobbs, K.C.V.O., O.B.E.),
Chairman of the Portland Club and head of a big company, carried
a good deal of weight. However, tournament players are not, for the
most part, great respecters of persons. A man may make a million
by his own efforts, but if he cannot play the dummy he is an ass.
Thus the T.B.A. events and Congresses continued to be well supported. In time a unified programme was agreed with the E.B.U.,
in which the main T.B.A. events were retained. It is not much remem-
bered now, but the Waddington Cup for Masters Pairs, the Richard
Lederer Memorial Cup, Crockford's Cup, the Anne Reese Cup, the
Two Stars, and many other Eastbourne and London events, were
originally T.B.A. promotions.

The T.B.A. venture was professionally very useful to me because
it led directly to a long series of broadcasts. In 1946 I acted as commentator for a live programme on the Lederer Cup, and when
Network Three was established the first press announcement by the
head of the Network mentioned bridge.

After an experimental programme in which Harrison-Gray and I
both took part, there was a meeting at Broadcasting House, attended
by S. J. de Lotbinière, the director of Outside Broadcasts, Stewart
Macpherson, Gray, Harold Selby and myself. Stewart Macpherson,
a Canadian and primarily a sports commentator, had made a great
reputation when acting as chairman of 'Twenty Questions', and it
was supposed that he would give a lift to the bridge programmes. It
soon became evident that Gray and I were not going to work in
harness. I wanted the broadcasts to be tied up with the T.B.A. Gray
would not agree. After an acrimonious discussion during which the
BBC men were obviously thinking 'Heaven save us from these
bridge players', it was proposed that we should submit plans
independently for a series of programmes. As it turned out, there
was no contest, one reason being that Gray and Stewart Macpherson
didn't hit it off. Stewart took his role as seriously as any actor and
you had to play up to him; Harold Selby was a master at this.

From this beginning, 'Bridge on the Air' continued with occasional breaks for about 12 years. Stewart Macpherson was succeeded by Henry Riddell, and later I introduced the programmes myself. Harold Franklin became my regular partner in the enterprise, his genial Yorkshire voice contrasting well with my more academic tone.

Harold and I did a paperback book on the series, entitled *The Best of Bridge on the Air*. This contained much first-class material but was not well circulated. Here are some excerpts from a section dealing with general topics that were discussed in 'Bridge Forum'. The questions were addressed to a panel and the answers are a distillation of the panel's opinions.

Luck and the Law of Averages

Q.   Some people say there is no such thing as lucky and unlucky players. Do you agree? In my club, certainly, some players seem to be luckier than others.

A.   Certainly some players *seem* to be luckier than others. No doubt, this is to some extent a subjective impression. When a bad or wild player has a run of cards everybody notices it.

Most players who think they hold less than their fair share of good cards are deluded. Nevertheless, we do not take the austere view that cards average out for everyone in the course of a period. The so-called law of averages does not require that they should. If you spin the roulette wheel 1,000 times it is consistent with mathematical expectancy that there should be runs for both red and black. So, in the wheel of life, it is normal to expect that some should be luckier at cards than others.

Men and Women at Bridge

Q.   Why do men play so much better than women?

A.   That is rather a loaded question, isn't it? Shall we break it into two parts: Do men play better than women? If so, why?

As to the first part, there is no doubt that at the higher levels there are many more good man players than good woman players. In the middle range it is a different story. The average woman club player is at least as good as the average man, and the biggest 'menaces' are invariably men.

As to why there are few women who excel, a partial reason may be that women who have the necessary brains tend to apply themselves to more serious occupations. For the rest, one can only beg the question and say that women do not possess the necessary qualities, either intellectual or temperamental. It is the same at chess.

Card Sense

Q.   Is there such a thing as card sense, and how do you define it?
A.   Of course there is such a thing as card sense. People who are good at one card game tend to be good at others of completely different kind and, as everybody knows, there are clever people who are useless at cards. The converse is not entirely true: most people who are top class at bridge have good minds.

We do not think it practicable to define card sense in any terms but its own. Card sense is a real and independent thing, like a sense of humour or a sense of direction, and if you try to break it up into components you will find that you run into a host of exceptions.

The Vanity of Bridge Players

Q.   Why do most bridge players think they play so much better than they do? And does it matter, anyway?
A.   It certainly is a bit of a mystery why so many players have false ideas about their prowess. Every 24 handicap golfer thinks he plays better than another 24 handicap golfer, but he knows he can't beat a 12 handicap player without some strokes. Yet at bridge you could pick out at every club several pairs of players, each of whom was certain beyond doubt that he was far superior to the other. The obvious explanation, though it doesn't seem to be a complete explanation, is that individual form cannot be assessed as it can at other games. Players who consistently lose are free to think that they are consistently unlucky.

That brings us to the second part of your question—does it matter? Obviously not, in the larger scale of things, but here again we meet a phenomenon that is easier to observe than to explain. For some reason, bridge engages the *amour propre* of most people more actively than almost any enterprise in life. Let us take it as a compliment to the game that players are so keen to assert themselves.

Husbands and Wives at Bridge

Q.   Why do many husbands and wives, who are normally most affectionate with one another, quarrel at the bridge table?

A.   This ties up with the previous question. Players like to win and tend to blame their partners, at least inwardly, when things go wrong. It is not surprising that husbands and wives, liberated from the normal social restraints, are more forthright in their criticisms.

Freak Deals

Q.   I wonder whether you have any opinion to express about the intermittent reports of complete suits being dealt to all four players at the table. All seem well attested, yet I read somewhere that if everybody in the world spent all day dealing cards it would be thousands of years before such a hand might be expected to turn up.

A.   We find it easier to believe in a breakdown of human veracity somewhere along the line. What is so puzzling is the Great Gap. Few players have ever held a suit of eleven or twelve cards, let alone thirteen. Furthermore, it is many million times more likely that a complete suit should be dealt to one player than to four. There have been at least a dozen reports of such a miracle, many of them on April 1! We suspect that in most cases the players were deluded by a practical joker, or conceivably that there was some connection with the arrangement of a new pack of cards, not shuffled.

Improving Your Game

Q.   What is the best way to improve? Through books, or by taking lessons, or by practice?

A.   We would be the last to decry the work of teachers and bridge schools. Nor do we underestimate the value of books, having contributed our quota of those. But the best single way to improve is to play with and against better players. In most sports it is practically impossible to rise far above the standard in which one normally plays, and that is especially true of bridge. The concentration of first-class players in a few centres is proof of that. To make big improvement you need to acquire technical knowledge from books and then to play in tournaments—better still, in clubs—where you will meet strong players.

People often ask me nowadays why I don't 'get bridge on television'. I have tried, of course, but it is an extremely frustrating business. To begin with, you have to get past the outermost gate where you receive a standard reply to the effect that your interesting suggestion is being considered. If eventually you succeed in making contact with someone who has influence you have to fight against two misconceptions: that bridge of necessity lacks visual and human interest, and that a bridge programme will lead to a mass turn-off in the industrial belt where intellectual pastimes are not a part of life.

Soon after the inception of BBC 2, which was supposed to cater for 'special interests' and now interprets that duty by dispensing the fifth re-run of ancient cowboy films, I made fair progress with one of the executives. The point was reached at which he was due to come to lunch and look at various outline scripts I had done for 'Bridge on the Air'. He asked if he could bring with him a well-known sports commentator who was said to be interested in the project. I thought this was a bad sign, and so it proved. The sports commentator had an idea for the programme. Briefly, it was that the bidding and play of a hand should be seen entirely from the angle of myself, the expert. I would pick up my cards and express my thoughts about them; as bids were made, I would say how they affected my hand; the same procedure would be followed throughout the play.

This may seem quite a bright method of presentation, but I could see at least three things wrong with it. Firstly, such a programme would of necessity be artificial and rehearsed. Throughout the run of 'Bridge on the Air', whenever any of the participants had to make a decision or express an opinion, there was nothing false or rehearsed about it. Secondly, the type of programme suggested would call for the play of 52 cards. This is tolerable on radio only if the programme has been pre-recorded and a diagram of the hand has appeared in the *Radio Times*; on television it is death, because only regular players can follow the play of an entire hand. Thirdly, there would be no suspense, no human interest; all the attention would be on my analysis.

I said it was an interesting suggestion, I would like to put it to the test alongside some other possible programmes. This was an inadequate response, of course. Worse, I offended this BBC narcissist by expressing a criticism of a sports programme with which he was associated. In due course I received a letter containing the asinine comment that it had been found impossible to devise a programme on bridge that would interest housewives who did not play the game.

In recent years the ITV has shown more inclination than the BBC to present bridge programmes. In one case they approached someone with no professional background at all; much excitement was generated, but the project never reached the screen. There has been one instructional series, presented at an unfashionable hour. A TV 'pro' and dummy actors who did not begin to look like card players ploughed through a prepared script. I thought it was terrible.

six

ANTI-DISCOVERY

The five years after the war were a rather lucky period for me in a professional sense. In quite a short time I made a reputation for myself as author, player, promoter of tournaments and broadcaster.

Anyone who looked at the long list of books to my name might think that here was an industrious toiler who made it his business to write a new book every year. It has not been like that at all.

Reese on Play, which was published in 1948 and did more than any other book to establish my reputation, came about in the following way. My brother, a master at Wellington, had done two history books for Edward Arnold, who are primarily educational publishers (Kennedy's *Latin Primer*, for example). The head of the firm, B. W. Fagan, was interested in bridge and invited me to submit copy for a book. I sent him the draft for a chapter on squeeze play, and *Reese on Play* resulted. Seven years later I suggested to the same firm that my *Observer* articles might make a good book, with the title, *Observations on Bridge*. 'Your public will expect something new from you', was the reply, and that led to *The Expert Game*. The starting-point for the *Bridge Player's Dictionary* was a phone call from an American publisher I had never met, and the same firm chartered *Play Bridge With Reese* and *Develop Your Bidding Judgment*. Both my Penguin books were the result of external suggestion. It has been the same all along.

In recent years I have done a number of collaborations and adaptations. The books I have written with Albert Dormer have been partnership enterprises in the fullest sense. We generally start on different sections of a book, then exchange drafts several times till at the finish we scarcely know ourselves who did the groundwork for which chapter. The benefit of this method is most clearly seen, I think, in *The Complete Book of Bridge*.

My three main journalistic jobs all came along within a few years of one another, and there was a fortuitous element about these too. I don't mean that I was less than well qualified, but such appointments do not always go on merit. In the early days especially, editors were well pleased if they could find a member of their own staff to do the bridge column: it saved money and they could rely on professional service.

Dr Melville Smith, who had been the *Evening News* correspondent for many years, died soon after the war and was succeeded by his friend and collaborator, Alex Hasler. When Hasler died, the job became open. One day Hubert Phillips was lunching with an old friend, L. F. Lampitt, features editor of the *News*. Lampitt remarked to him, 'I have had about 30 applications for this bridge job, I don't know what to do.' 'Is Terence Reese one of them?' asked Hubert. 'If so, you needn't look any further.'

One evening about a year later I took part in a television programme on the European Championship, which had just been held in Paris. Skid, who was one of the participants, was much bothered by the studio lights, which generated an uncomfortable heat. The next morning I had a phone call from Gray's wife, Stella, with the very sad news that Skid had died during the night. Stella was speaking from Skid's flat in Bickenhall Mansions and his wife, Carmel, came to the phone. I asked if there was anything I could do to help on the professional side—for example, by ringing Skid's agent and letting them know at the *Observer*, where Skid had a column. The *Observer* asked me to write a piece about him for the following Sunday. In this I described the television date:

He had a new tie for the occasion, buttercup yellow. 'Thought was Technicolor', he said.

I commented on his distinctive style—the omission of the personal pronoun, the disregard for syntax—and ended:

His humour always touched the human comedy, but never with malice. For example:
At a pre-war Congress a lady who held an ace and was on lead against seven no trumps neither doubled nor led the ace. The contract was made and the story of the double omission quickly went the rounds. It was Skid who pointed out that she must be acquitted on at least one count. If she was not going to lead the ace, he said, she was quite right not to double.

The assistant editor, J. C. Trewin, now a colleague on the *Lady*, was kind enough to reply, 'Thank you for the piece about S. J. Simon. It could not be better.' I was asked to write the column 'for the next few weeks' and have done so ever since.

When Skid's wife, Carmel, and her sister, Mollie, first appeared on the bridge scene, the two Misses Withers invariably propped up the field in the Tuesday night duplicates at Lederers. Both married expert players and both, within a few years, played for Britain in the European Championship. Carmel was a handsome and brilliant girl who could dash off the sort of crossword where none of the rest of us could solve a single clue. She was lost without Skid and died within the year.

Mollie married Niel Furse, a skilful and enigmatic player who took part in many big matches before the war. He was a finalist in the 1947 Gold Cup, a needle match between Acol and Baron teams, which the Barons just won. The final rounds were played at the Cheltenham Congress, and because of the crowded programme the semi-final was played on the Saturday morning. A veteran resident of the hotel, forced to move from his favourite corner, muttered darkly about the iniquity of playing bridge at such an hour.

'I cannot agree with you, sir', said Niel, with a waggle of his sandy moustache. 'The morning is the right time for bridge. Afternoons should be reserved exclusively for horse racing.'

Niel made another memorable remark. Of a pair who had been at odds with one another during the first half of a match: 'They played the second half back to back.'

People often say, 'You write for the *Observer* (or the *Evening News*), you must know so-and-so.' I never do. My only contact is with whoever collates outside contributions and sees them through the press. This is seldom a bridge player. Once when I was abroad I had a cable from the *Evening News*: COPY JULY 7 STATES SOUTH LOST TWO ACES STOP SOUTH HASNT GOT TWO ACES. So, how could he mislay them?

My other writing job, on the *Lady*, came a few years later. This, too, I owed to Hubert, who had previously written the column himself.

The years after the war were also a successful time for me in a playing sense. I began to play with Boris Schapiro in about 1944 and we immediately struck sparks from one another. To play with someone so intense was good for my game and we had similar views on bidding. For the first European Championship after the war, Copenhagen in 1948, the selectors arranged a match of 400 boards between the leading Acol group and the leading CAB group.

(CAB, Two *C*lubs, *A*ce responses, *B*lackwood, was the standard system at the Hamilton Club.) This proved a very close affair and the experience was of value to all the players. A team of seven (allowed in those days) was drawn from both sides: Gray, Simon, Schapiro and myself, Konstam, Dodds and Rayne. The team to fear in those days was Sweden, with Kock-Werner, Lilliehook-Anulf, and later Wohlin. We finished level on victory points and won because our matchpoint quotient was better than theirs. At Paris the following year we beat the Swedes by one victory point. Italy played in the championship for the first time, finishing fifth; the signs were there.

Eddie Rayne, now Shoemaker to the Queen, was too busy to play in Paris and was replaced by Meredith. I played several sessions with Meredith, partly because of a silly affair which resulted in Schapiro and Konstam being suspended for three matches. It was very hot in the Closed Room and Konstam, unable to find a waiter, went out for a few moments to get a drink at the bar. When there, he exchanged a word with Schapiro, who had been playing, or watching, in the Open Room. This encounter was reported and the players were suspended. Since it was fully accepted that the remark they exchanged had nothing to do with the match, the penalty seemed to us to reflect excessive zeal on the part of the officials. We thought they might have paid more attention to the time-keeping. The afternoon session was supposed to begin at 2.30, but if you were so foolish as to go to the playing room at that hour you would see nothing to suggest that a bridge tournament was even planned: not a duplicate board, not a scorer or director. It was like the French races, where the timing of a race for 2.30 means that the jockeys put their socks on at that hour. I must say, however, that when the Pairs Olympiad was held at Cannes a few years later, the organization was excellent.

Guy Ramsey, editor of the *Contract Bridge Journal*, hailed the victories at Copenhagen and Paris in these terms: 'Our thanks go to them [the players] not merely from bridge players but from patriots who take pride in national achievement.' Such high-flown sentiments were typical of his style. One of his preoccupations concerned the Camrose* trials, which at that time were held only for provincial players. It was unjust, Guy contended, that the winners of

---

* The Camrose Trophy is the home international series.

provincial trials should make the team automatically, whereas in London 'If one be not a Gray or a Reese, or on the international squad at the very least, one can be a ranking expert for a decade and still not achieve the right to play for one's country.' The story had a happy ending. London players not on the 'panel' were included in the trials and eventually Guy was 'Capped for England'.

Writing in the *European Bridge Review*, Herman Filarski related this deal from Britain *v* Holland at Copenhagen:

South dealer
Love all

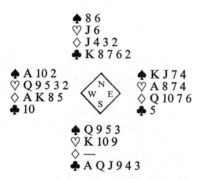

```
                    ♠ 8 6
                    ♡ J 6
                    ◇ J 4 3 2
                    ♣ K 8 7 6 2
  ♠ A 10 2                         ♠ K J 7 4
  ♡ Q 9 5 3 2          N          ♡ A 8 7 4
  ◇ A K 8 5        W       E      ◇ Q 10 7 6
  ♣ 10                 S          ♣ 5
                    ♠ Q 9 5 3
                    ♡ K 10 9
                    ◇ —
                    ♣ A Q J 9 4 3
```

Schapiro and I were East-West and the bidding was on one note:

South	West	North	East
1 ♣	Dble	3 ♣	4 ♣
5 ♣	No	No	Dble
No	No	No	

Declarer won the trump lead in hand, crossed to ♣ K and led a low spade from the table. I went up with the king and led a low heart. Placing me with ♠ A K, the declarer made the wrong guess in hearts and went two down.

I mention this hand because an almost identical anti-discovery play by Garozzo in a world championship match at Guajara 25 years later received a good deal of publicity. The object of an anti-discovery play is to mislead the declarer about the lie of one suit so that he will misguess the lie in another. Here is a more striking example:

♠ 10 5
♡ J 9 6
◇ Q 10 8
♣ Q 10 7 4 2

♠ Q 7 2
♡ 8 3
◇ A 9 5 3
♣ A J 6 5

♠ A 8 4
♡ 7 5
◇ K J 6 2
♣ K 9 8 3

♠ K J 9 6 3
♡ A K Q 10 4 2
◇ 7 4
♣ —

South, who has indicated a pronounced major two-suiter, plays in 4 ♡. West leads ◇ A and follows with ◇ 3 to East's jack. It should be clear to East that the contract may depend on a spade guess. At trick 3 he should lay down ♣ K. If South places East with ♣ A K he will go wrong in spades. I have an idea that more attention to anti-discovery plays will be one of the main developments in play during the next few years.

TRIALS—AND TRIBULATIONS

In any account of bridge history, trials, and the selection of international teams, are a recurring theme. Almost every year 'something' happens—a protest, a withdrawal, a selectorial rebuke.

Going ahead in time, when Albert Dormer was editing the *British Bridge World* there was frequent correspondence about methods of team selection. On one occasion Frank Farrington, a Lancashire player and tournament director, Edmund Phillips from Cheshire, Harry Ingram and Dormer himself all expressed views on the matter. I joined in the argument with the following letter:

In the May issue you publish three letters on the subject of team selection and add a number of editorial observations. What strikes me about these letters is that none of them is addressed to the question of what the selection committee is really trying to do, or should be trying to do. Perhaps it is not surprising, because the selectors themselves have seemed on occasions to have confused notions.

There is talk in these letters about justice being seen to be done (Farrington), giving all players their opportunity (Farrington), laying down the procedure for trials in advance (Phillips), avoiding heart-burning among players who might reasonably expect to participate (Ingram), maintaining the prestige of the governing bodies (Ingram), it being wrong to have a different method each year (Editor), not wishing to encourage *prima donna* attitudes (Phillips), bringing out a sound scheme unhampered by interested parties (Ingram), not letting the minority with special interests wag the selectorial tail (Editor, *passim*).

Most of these objectives are, to my mind, irrelevant and red herrings. Could we not approach the matter more logically and purposefully by asking two questions:

1. What are the selectors trying to do?

2. How are they to achieve it?

You might think that the answer to (1) was self-evident—choose the best team. But if you look at the excerpts quoted above, you will see that many other objectives are brought into the reckoning. Do the public at large (who foot the bill) consider it important to 'Keep the players happy'? I don't think so. It is the players on the fringe—the 'interested parties'—who talk in these terms and sometimes succeed in deflecting the selectors from their proper task.

Now let us pass to the second question posed above, and to clear our minds let us begin with a hypothesis:

Suppose that the selectors were like football managers or baseball coaches, and that it were worth £5,000 to each of them to send a winning team to the next championship, what would they do?

To name just two of the fatuous suggestions that are made every year, would they determine to send the winners of the Gold Cup, just like that? Don't make me laugh! Would they hold a series of pairs trials and abide by the results? Don't make me cry!

What they would probably do is decide that certain players were worth their place and ought not to be left out, and to complete the team they would hold team trials, perhaps requiring the 'probables' to take part. Then they would choose the final team on the basis of the form displayed—not strictly on the results.

In a sentence, the proper function of trials is *to aid the selectors*. If the selectors are then going to worry about hurt feelings they should go in for social work, and if they commit themselves to the result of a trial they are abrogating their responsibility.

Bert Dormer had the last word with this little rhyme:

> *The thought of holding trials*
> *For players on the fringe*
> *Gives our number one selection*
> *A most uneasy twinge.*

Back now to 1950, when the European Championship was due to be held in Brighton. Early in the year it was announced by the B.B.L. that Boris Schapiro and I had been nominated as 'Probables' and that trials would be held to complete the team. Mobbs himself informed us of this decision, remarking a little mysteriously that he and the B.B.L. did not accept certain comments that had been made about the team in Paris. I didn't know what he was talking about and didn't inquire; Boris and I, in our different ways, are quite capable of offending people who are not used to our sense of humour. However, when the team for Brighton was finally announced, after trials had been held, we were not included. I remember Iain Macleod giving me the news, with a considerable sense of shock (his, not mine).

No explanation was given. Some people recalled the differences between the B.B.L. and the T.B.A. in the late 1940s, others made the ready assumption that Boris and I had somehow blotted our copybook since being nominated as 'Probables'. Guy Ramsey, in the *Contract Bridge Journal*, advanced this theory:

One reason is that, deplorably in our view (and the B.B.L.'s) a

split occurred between the members of the Paris team which resolved what had been an entity into two apparently irreconcilable
factions. It had been our intention to elaborate on these 'impon-
derables', dotting the i's and crossing the t's in our often criticised
fashion.

Guy didn't do so, which was probably wise, because this was
utter nonsense. No doubt Gray had some grievance—he always had
—but there were no factions. Simon, Dodds and Rayne were people
with whom it would be impossible to quarrel, and the foibles of the
rest of us were well known and not taken seriously. Meredith, who
had been chosen for the Brighton team, sought an interview with
Mobbs and asked why Boris and I had been dropped in this fashion.
Mobbs did not feel obliged to account for the B.B.L.'s actions and
told Meredith that if he did not play at Brighton his international
career might be permanently prejudiced. Plum, as obstinate as
twenty mules, was not the type to be impressed by a threat. He withdrew from the team and was replaced by Jack Marx.

There was an extremely close finish at Brighton, at least five teams
having a chance to win when the last round began. Britain was
down to France at half-time but recovered to win, and thanks to
some other matches turning out favourably for us the team won
with the low total of 14 victory points out of 20. Britain thus qualified for the Bermuda Bowl. At the banquet Mobbs announced that
should there be any withdrawals 'the selection committee would
surely consider the name of Mr Terence Reese as a potential candidate, if a suitable partner could be found for him'. I did not have the
satisfaction of spitting at this offer, for when Jack Marx withdrew
he was replaced by Joel Tarlo. The team made a fair start in the
Bermuda Bowl but finished last in a three-cornered affair.

For Venice the following year a long pairs trial was arranged, at
the end of which the leading pairs were to be formed into teams for
a further contest. The sensation this time was that Gray, who had
entered with Joel Tarlo, withdrew after the first round, announcing
his retirement from international competition. By so doing, he dis-
rupted the trials and left Joel high and dry. Apart from saying that
his withdrawal had nothing to do with the current trial, he would
give no explanation. In January the following year the B.B.L.
announced that Gray would not be considered for selection in the

team to represent Britain in Dublin. As it turned out, he did not play for Britain again until Oslo in 1958.

The team for Venice (Gardener-L. Tarlo, Truscott-D'Unienville, Reese-Schapiro), with Iain Macleod as non-playing captain, made a poor start but recovered well to finish a close third to Italy and Austria. For once we had a better quotient than any team, including Italy.

Gray attended the championship but stayed in a different hotel and we saw nothing of him. In a long account for the *European Bridge Review* he wrote of the team that 'after deplorable tactics at the start they pulled themselves together with some big wins against half-hearted opposition and beat Italy when the outcome was immaterial and the Italian players (minus their best pair) had indulged in an all-night celebration of their victory'. He followed these remarks by saying that he had been 'unable to make more than token appearances in the playing room . . . I saw exactly one hand played through to the end'.

I don't think the players minded all this, but Harry Ingram, who had succeeded Guy as editor of the *Contract Bridge Journal*, was full of patriotic ire. It was certainly a strange performance by Gray all the way along. He had an excellent sense of humour about most things, but one had the impression that he thought people were out to withhold credit from him, and this appeared to colour his actions.

The European Championship in 1952 was played at Dun Laoghaire, a seaside resort about eight miles from Dublin. The selectors on this occasion organized a long series of team trials, requiring the players to form up in various ways and not committing themselves to choose strictly according to results. Expert assessors were appointed to study the form. All this was sensible enough, but the members of the committee, as Ewart Kempson put it in the *Bridge Magazine*, did not escape charges of incompetence, partisanship, favouritism, arson and insanity.

The trials dragged on for months and Meredith put himself out of court by declining to return from the South of France for the fifth weekend. The eventual team was Konstam-Dodds, L. Tarlo-Franklin, Reese-Schapiro, with Geoffrey Fell as non-playing captain.

The championship was played in two divisions that year, with a semi-final and final. It seemed a good idea to me, though it has never been repeated. The individual matches were longer, but the championship was shorter, which surely ought to be a consideration in the present straitened times.

We lost to Italy by 13 in the semi-final. The Swedes had consolation for their narrow defeats at Copenhagen and Paris when they just beat Italy in the final.

A distressing accident to one of our players provided a good example of team morale. Someone rushed into our hotel with the news that Louis Tarlo had fallen off a jetty into the sea and I said, 'What about Franklin?'

Are such remarks (or the reporting of them) taken too seriously? Harry Ingram was always writing about the supposed bickering and jealousy among the leading players.

Tarlo hurt his back in the accident and was unable to take any further part in the championship. 'My Louis has never been the same since', said his wife, Bea, in her deep-toned voice.

eight

THE NEW MEMBER

As a change from trials, championships and personalities, I recall in this chapter an aspect of my writing that is not widely known. It is possible that I think it is undervalued. There may be a suggestion here of the comedian who wants to play Hamlet, in reverse; the reader must judge.

Hubert Phillips invented a set of characters, headed by the pedagogic Mr Playbetter, whom he presented in the 'Annals of Ruff's Club'. When I succeeded him on *The Lady* I took over some of these characters, giving them more edge, and introduced some new ones, including a 'villain', Humphrey Hoosego. The articles I wrote for *The Lady* formed the substance of a book called *Bridge With Mr Playbetter*. This was published in 1952 and has long been out of print, though some of the episodes have been revived in magazines.

The episode below marks the first appearance of *Humphrey Hoosego*. The other main characters are:

Miss Trumpary, a no-nonsense type 'who scorned artificial aids alike to her complexion and her slam bidding'.

Commander Scroop, described by Hoosego as a 'pedantic ass'.

Janet Sloe, a mousey little thing, easily flustered.

The New Member

'What beats me', said Commander Scroop for the twentieth time, 'is how the committee ever came to elect the fellow. I can't imagine what they were thinking about.'

'You know how difficult it was', said Mrs Niceways. 'When Lady Glum said at the last meeting that her nephew was coming to stay with her, and that he was so keen on bridge and such a good player, what could we do but elect him? After all, she is President. Besides,' she added weakly, 'he is a good player, isn't he?'

'Jolly lucky, that's all', said Scroop.

Humphrey Hoosego was the new member's name. In less than a week he had made himself thoroughly unpopular with everyone except his aunt.

As to his luck, the session that led up to Scroop's outburst had certainly found him in fortunate vein. After winning four rubbers in a row he had cut Miss Trumpary against Scroop and Miss Sloe. His side won the first game with a slam and was several hundred up above the line when this hand was dealt by Miss Sloe:

Miss Trumpary
♠ K 9 3
♡ —
◇ A K Q 8 6 4
♣ K J 5 2

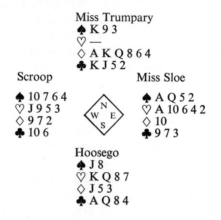

Scroop
♠ 10 7 6 4
♡ J 9 5 3
◇ 9 7 2
♣ 10 6

Miss Sloe
♠ A Q 5 2
♡ A 10 6 4 2
◇ 10
♣ 9 7 3

Hoosego
♠ J 8
♡ K Q 8 7
◇ J 5 3
♣ A Q 8 4

The bidding was brief but lively:

South	West	North	East
1 ♣	No	2 ◇	No
2 ♡	No	6 ♣	Dble
No	No	No	

Scroop led ◇ 2 and dummy's hand went down.

'No use beating about the bush with my hand', said Miss Trumpary, who did not espouse the Blackwood convention.

Hoosego won the first trick in his own hand. He saw that it would be difficult, owing to lack of entries, to ruff two hearts and draw trumps. A better plan, he decided, would be to draw trumps, discard his spades on dummy's diamonds, and give up a trick to ♡ A. Assuming a 3–2 break in trumps, that would bring in twelve tricks by way of four trumps, one ruff, six diamonds and one heart.

So he drew trumps in three rounds and ran off the diamonds. This was the position when the last diamond was led:

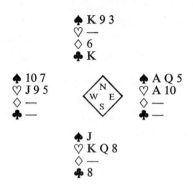

```
            ♠ K 9 3
            ♡ —
            ◇ 6
            ♣ K
♠ 10 7                      ♠ A Q 5
♡ J 9 5                     ♡ A 10
◇ —                         ◇ —
♣ —                         ♣ —
            ♠ J
            ♡ K Q 8
            ◇ —
            ♣ 8
```

East discarded a heart and Hoosego had his finger on ♠ J when it dawned on him that, with only one trump left in his hand, his plan of setting up a trick in hearts was not going to work. So he threw a heart and held on to ♠ J. A small spade followed from dummy, won by East's queen.

Miss Sloe was now in a most embarrassing position. Whichever ace she played, she was bound to establish declarer's twelfth trick. She played ♡ A, dummy ruffed, and South made the last two tricks with ♣ 8 and ♡ K.

'That was the only way to make it', exclaimed Hoosego exultantly. 'It's no use throwing all my spades. You beat it if you lead a spade, Admiral.'

'Indeed, I hoped you would lead a spade, partner', said Miss Sloe. 'Deborah called diamonds, you know.'

'I appreciate that', said Scroop. 'I rather assumed that yours was a Lightner double, asking me to make a surprise lead. I placed you with a void in diamonds.'

'I don't know about lightning doubles,' said Miss Sloe, 'but if you can't double a slam call with two aces, when can you?'

Scroop wisely took this to be a rhetorical question not demanding an answer.

In the next episode the characters are:

Miss Trumpary, whom we have already met.

General Braveblood, 'who had the air of weather-beaten vacuity that is characteristic of high military officers'.

Mrs Bland-Beamish, a chatterbox.

Walter Hurry, an insurance man who belied his profession by making the wildest calls. On the deal below he had little scope.

A Skilful Unblock

Miss Trumpary and General Braveblood were opposed to Mrs Bland-Beamish and Mr Hurry. Early in the rubber Miss Trumpary dealt herself the following hand at love all:

♠ —
♡ K Q 10 8 5 2
◇ 10 9 8 6 3
♣ K 4

This was a sound opening bid in her estimation, but she knew that her partner's valour in the field was not matched by audacity at the card table and that he would expect the standard $2\frac{1}{2}$ quick tricks.

'No Bid', she declared, interrupting the flow of Mrs Bland-Beamish's conversation.

'I took it straight back', Mrs Bland-Beamish was saying to the General, 'and I said: "Butcher, do you call that a tournedos? I can only tell you . . ."'

'No Bid!' said Miss Trumpary again. 'No Bid! NO BID!'

'What's that?' asked Mrs Bland-Beamish. 'Three No Bids? I have nothing to say', and she threw in her cards.

Luckily they were face downwards and the General restored them with a gallant gesture.

'Where was I?' asked Mrs Bland-Beamish, when the position had been explained to her.

'At the butcher's', said Hurry.

'That's right', she went on. 'As I was saying . . .'

'NO BID!' said Miss Trumpary.

'Oh, very well', said Mrs Bland-Beamish. 'I passed before, I suppose I must do so again.'

This was the full deal:

General Braveblood
♠ 10 8 6 5 4 2
♡ A 7 3
◇ A K Q
♣ A

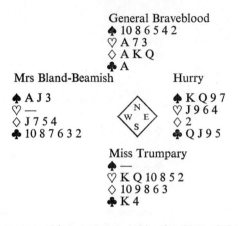

Mrs Bland-Beamish

♠ A J 3
♡ —
◇ J 7 5 4
♣ 10 8 7 6 3 2

Hurry

♠ K Q 9 7
♡ J 9 6 4
◇ 2
♣ Q J 9 5

Miss Trumpary
♠ —
♡ K Q 10 8 5 2
◇ 10 9 8 6 3
♣ K 4

My partner would open 2 ♠ on this, the General thought to himself, but the spades are very poor. So he opened 1 ♠.

Miss Trumpary responded with 2 ♡. The General had a straightforward raise to 4 ♡, but he preferred 3 ◇. As it happened, this made the slam easier to bid. Miss Trumpary jumped to 5 ◇, the the General retreated to 5 ♡ and Miss Trumpary bid 6 ♡. Mr Hurry, who always liked to be in the game, doubled and all passed. The bidding had been:

South	West	North	East
No	No	1 ♠	No
2 ♡	No	3 ◇	No
5 ◇	No	5 ♡	No
6 ♡	Dble	No	No
No			

Having been reminded of the contract and assured that it was her lead, Mrs Bland-Beamish laid down ♠ A. Miss Trumpary ruffed, drew trumps in four rounds and then played off the top diamonds. It was a shock when Hurry showed out on the second diamond, for the position then was:

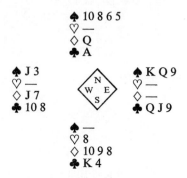

♠ 10 8 6 5
♥ —
♦ Q
♣ A

♠ J 3   ♠ K Q 9
♥ —   ♥ —
♦ J 7   ♦ —
♣ 10 8   ♣ Q J 9

♠ —
♥ 8
♦ 10 9 8
♣ K 4

Miss Trumpary played off ♦ Q and ♣ A. To return to her hand she had to use her last trump. She cashed ♣ K, but Mrs Bland-Beamish made the last two tricks with ♦ J and ♠ J, Hurry having kept a club as his last card.

'That's funny', said Mrs Bland-Beamish. 'You doubled, and I made both tricks to put them down.'

'There was nothing wrong with the contract, I fancy', remarked the General. 'Both suits broke badly. Bad luck, partner!'

'Fiddlesticks!' said Miss Trumpary. 'Played it badly, that's all. Your deal, Lavinia!' She cut the cards with a bang.

Mr Hurry played the rest of the rubber in a daze, wondering how the contract could have been made. He reconstructed the deal later and showed it to Mr Playbetter.

'The play is very easy to miss', commented the maestro, 'and we must give full credit to Miss Trumpary for realizing she had made a mistake. The hand looks easy until West shows out on the first round of trumps. Then there is a danger of declarer losing control if the diamonds also break badly. That is what happened, and this is how it could have been avoided:

'When in dummy after the second round of hearts, declarer must play off ♦ A and ♣ A. Then ♦ K and ♦ Q are discarded on the fourth heart and the ♣ K. Declarer gives up a trick to ♦ J, but she still has a trump for entry and no more tricks are lost.'

'Jolly clever, that', said Hurry, 'I must show this hand to Alfred Bulldozer. He might want to have a bet on it.' Alfred Bulldozer, a scrap metal merchant, was a crony of Hoosego's.

Although several of the characters were borrowed from Hubert, for the general tone I owed more to two books written in Auction days. I wonder who remembers *Mrs Pottleton's Bridge Parties*, and its sequel, by a writer named Hugh Tuite? The only characters I recall by name, apart from the hostess and her husband, are 'old Mrs Vering', who always redoubled, and 'Miss Arden', the blushing postmistress. S. J. Simon also used fictional characters, more sharply delineated in a bridge sense, and in modern times Victor Mollo has had great success with his anthropomorphic animals.

nine

TWO AUSPICIOUS BEGINNINGS

Looking through the *Contract Bridge Journal* of May 1953, I was surprised to see a paragraph to the effect that, after the first round of trials for Helsinki, I had asked not to be considered for the team. I know I didn't play in the championship that year, but why depart after playing in a trial? Was I sulking because my team lost that first match? No, that's not one of my weaknesses. I asked Boris if he could remember what it was all about.

'Of course', he said. 'We both played in trials, but only to provide opposition. You played with Hans Leist. We told the selectors at the beginning of the season that we were not candidates. You couldn't tear yourself away from White City. Besides, you thought it would be freezing cold in Helsinki.' My alleged insularity is a standard joke between us.

He was probably right about the other reason. Apart from one or two important events, I played very little bridge at that time. At Crockford's I played poker and, when the craze was on, canasta. I never cared much for poker as a game, but the good player's advantage is higher than it can ever be at bridge. In club poker, as it was played then, all you needed to do was play to the odds. There were several bad gamblers around, until the casino games drew them off. Canasta, on the other hand, I enjoyed very much. In 1951 Colin Harding (Macleod's partner in the first University match) and I played a public match at Selfridges against American expert Johnny Crawford and his partner, which we managed to win.

I spent all my evenings at the greyhound tracks, which accounts for the reference to White City. I had always been very keen on this sport. Even in Oxford days I used to slip away twice a week, to the Reading track. It was especially interesting to have a share in a book, supplying capital to a bookmaker who had a pitch. This was fairly profitable in summer, hard work in the winter. One day at West Ham we operated in a howling gale and half-way through the meeting the firm's umbrella was blown inside out. The bookmaker, the tic-tac, the bagman, the runner, the clerk, Boris and myself had to form a sort of Conga line to prevent the 'joint' from being carried away into the empty terraces. At this moment there was the melancholy rattle of a collecting box and a voice saying, 'Flood Relief! Your contributions please, gentlemen, for Flood Relief.' Iniquitous taxes have now made the game too difficult.

The team that eventually went to Helsinki consisted of Albert Rose (nephew of Lederer's partner, Willie Rose) and Nico Gardener, Konstam and Dodds, Swinnerton-Dyer and Mrs Fleming. Swinnie's partner in the trials had been unable to go, and this third pair was regarded with some misgiving by the stay-at-home professionals. However, they made a sensational debut when they were brought in for the second half against Norway and held these cards on their first board:

Mrs Fleming	Swinnerton-Dyer
♠ Q 2	♠ A K 10 9
♡ A J 9 8 6	♡ —
◇ J 6 3	◇ A K 7 5
♣ A K 9	♣ Q J 10 8 2

West	*East*
1 ♡	3 ♣
3 ♡	3 ♠
4 ♣	6 ♣
7 ♣	

West judged that if her partner could bid six, not knowing that she held A K of the trump suit, together with ♠ Q to fill in the side suits, there must be a good play for seven. Still, it must have been a fairly nerve-racking decision. I don't know how the opposing cards lay, but it strikes me that the best line of play is to cash two diamonds early on. If the queen falls, declarer needs to ruff only one spade; if not, he must take the risk of playing three top spades for a diamond discard. Anyway, the grand slam was made, while the Norwegians stopped in six. The team did very well, finishing a close second to France.

As European champions, France qualified to meet America in a world championship match at Monte Carlo early in 1954. The American team, which had won a round-robin event in the masters team championship, was Ellenby, Rosen, Steen, Bishop and Oakie, and Lew Mathe was imported as sixth man. Ellenby and Rosen had won the masters pairs as well, and Alfred Sheinwold, writing in the *Bridge Magazine*, gave us this foretaste of their skill:

East dealer
E-W vulnerable

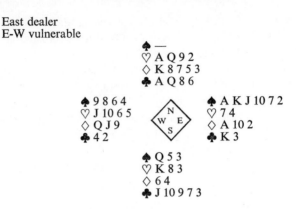

```
                      ♠ —
                      ♡ A Q 9 2
                      ◇ K 8 7 5 3
                      ♣ A Q 8 6
   ♠ 9 8 6 4                        ♠ A K J 10 7 2
   ♡ J 10 6 5          N            ♡ 7 4
   ◇ Q J 9         W       E        ◇ A 10 2
   ♣ 4 2               S            ♣ K 3
                      ♠ Q 5 3
                      ♡ K 8 3
                      ◇ 6 4
                      ♣ J 10 9 7 3
```

With Ellenby South and Rosen North, the bidding went:

South	West	North	East
—	—	—	1 ♠
No	2 ♠	Dble	4 ♠
No	No	4 NT	No
5 ♣	No	No	No

If Rosen was going to be so bold as to bid again over 4 ♠, a double, leaving partner more options, would perhaps have been a better choice than 4 NT.

Against 5 ♣ West certainly ought to have led a trump, but he made the unfortunate choice of ♡ J, which ran to the declarer's king. The play continued: finesse of ♡ 9; ♡ A, ruffed by East; ♠ K, ruffed in dummy; ♣ A, dropping the king; ♡ Q, South discarding a diamond; ◇ K, forcing East to win; and as East had no more trumps, the rest of the hand could be played as a crossruff.

This was a fine example of control and timing. It may seem as though, since he is intending to play East for ♣ K, South may as well lay down ♣ A after finessing ♡ 9; but then East declines to ruff ♡ A or ♡ Q, and when the defenders come in with a diamond they play a second round of trumps, leaving South a trick short.

Benjamin O. Johnson, President of the A.C.B.L. and non-playing captain of the American team, had made it known that his team would be free to play a few matches in Europe before returning home. Seizing on this opportunity, I induced Simpson's, of Piccadilly, to stage a match. The store paid the expenses of the visitors while in Britain. The Americans won at Monte Carlo, so came to Britain as world champions, but minus Rosen, who had to return home to pursue his law studies.

The home team consisted of Meredith, Konstam, Mayer, Schapiro, Reese. Leslie Dodds was invited, but business affairs intervened. Edward Mayer, less well known in the tournament world than the others, had long been regarded as an outstanding rubber-bridge player. His first book, *Money Bridge*, written when rationing was a recent memory, summed up a whole world of players in this phrase: 'If, like a grocer, you value your stock in points . . .'

A programme note implied that Mayer would be used as a kind of secret weapon, stating that he would be 'kept in reserve to come in with Konstam at critical stages of the match'. It didn't turn out like that, because things went swimmingly for our team from the start and we were able to play in various formations. On board 3 a psychic bomb by Meredith exploded right in the enemy camp.

East dealer
E-W vulnerable

```
                    ♠ K 8 5 3
                    ♡ —
                    ◇ K 5 4 3 2
                    ♣ K 10 4 3
  ♠ Q J 10 7 6                    ♠ A
  ♡ 5 3 2          N              ♡ K J 10 9 7
  ◇ Q          W       E          ◇ A 10 9 8
  ♣ A 9 8 6         S             ♣ Q 7 5
                    ♠ 9 4 2
                    ♡ A Q 8 6 4
                    ◇ J 7 6
                    ♣ J 2
```

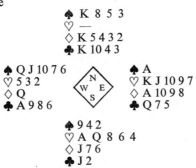

In the open room Mayer, sitting East, played quietly in 2 ♡ and made nine tricks. This was the bidding in Room 2:

South	West	North	East
Meredith	Oakie	Schapiro	Bishop
—	—	—	1 ♡
1 ♠ (!)	2 ♣	4 ♠	5 ♣
Dble	5 ♡	No	No
Dble	No	No	No

This was 800 down, so it was a gain of 940 for the home team.

Both American players have been blamed for their bids in Room 2, but I feel that the combination of circumstances was rather unlucky for them. West, obviously, might have doubled 1 ♠, but that seldom pays at the score. Probably the wisest course, especially if he suspected that South might be psyching, would have been to pass. East's 5 ♣ was calamitous in the result, but it is easy to imagine a different lie of the cards.

Plum's overcall of 1 ♠ was typical in two respects: most of his psychic bids were made around the spade suit, and he always liked to establish a psychological advantage early in a match. I remember how amused we all were at Eastbourne one year when an L.O.L. (bridge parlance for 'little old lady') bluffed him out of a game. 'She had an enormous bag full of knitting', he said. 'How could I think she was going to psyche?'

The editorial publicity for this match was the best that bridge had enjoyed since the early Culbertson matches. Perhaps because I was concerned with the promotional aspect, I made what the cricket commentators call 'an uncertain start', but I must have had my wits about me later when this hand was played:

East dealer
Love all

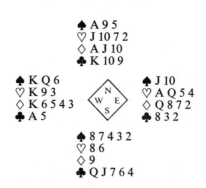

```
              ♠ A 9 5
              ♡ J 10 7 2
              ◇ A J 10
              ♣ K 10 9
♠ K Q 6                      ♠ J 10
♡ K 9 3          N           ♡ A Q 5 4
◇ K 6 5 4 3   W     E        ◇ Q 8 7 2
♣ A 5            S           ♣ 8 3 2
              ♠ 8 7 4 3 2
              ♡ 8 6
              ◇ 9
              ♣ Q J 7 6 4
```

In Room 1 Mathe played as West in 3 ◇ and made four after the lead of a low heart by North. This was the bidding in Room 2:

South Ellenby	West Reese	North Oakie	East Schapiro
—	—	—	No
No	1 NT	Dble	Redble
2 ♣	No	No	Dble
No	No	No	

We were lucky that South did not retreat to 2 ♠, for we might have doubled that also and could not have defeated it.

I led a low diamond against 2 ♣ doubled. Declarer went up with the ace and played ace and another spade. If partner's 10 and jack were to be believed, South had two five-card suits, so the defence was to force in diamonds. When I won the next spade I punched again, and this was the position:

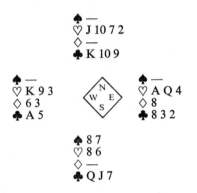

```
                    ♠ —
                    ♡ J 10 7 2
                    ◇ —
                    ♣ K 10 9
    ♠ —                            ♠ —
    ♡ K 9 3          N             ♡ A Q 4
    ◇ 6 3        W       E         ◇ 8
    ♣ A 5            S             ♣ 8 3 2
                    ♠ 8 7
                    ♡ 8 6
                    ◇ —
                    ♣ Q J 7
```

South could afford to lose the three top tricks, but no more. After some thought he led a low heart. East won and returned a trump, on which South played the 7. If I release ♣ A now, declarer is home. I had to play the 5, and when East won the next heart he led a second club. After ♣ A a red suit lead established a trump trick for partner. From the beginning of the hand, the defence had to be just so.

(If, in the diagram position, South leads a spade and ruffs with the 10, he can still be beaten. East wins the heart return and plays a club. Now if South plays low, so does West, but if South puts in the jack West plays the ace and returns the club.)

The Americans had no luck in this match and lost by a big margin. No doubt the balance of their team was upset by the absence of Rosen.

Later in the year the same team, with Rixi Markus in place of Meredith, won an international event at Monte Carlo. There was a sort of Pro-Am Individual at that tournament, with good cash prizes. For once in a way I was going well until the last set of boards, which I played with a typical Monte Carlo resident. After two poor results she played the final board in 4 ♡ doubled, which was cold, and went two down. At the end of the play she looked up, diamonds a-glitter, and said brightly:

'Tell me, Mr Reese, how would *you* have played that hand?'

'Differently.'

ten

A SLIGHT MYSTERY

For Montreux in 1954 the trials consisted of two matches of 100 boards each between Louis Tarlo's team, holders of the Gold Cup, and our usual quintet of Dodds, Konstam, Meredith, Schapiro, Reese. We won the first match very easily, to the astonishment of Norman Squire, author of *The Theory of Bidding*, who had described the Gold Cup team's equipment as 'careful, modern, scientific and exploratory'—the highest praise in his vocabulary. He found their performance in this match 'quite mystifying'. The second match was closer, but we won again. As a sixth player we needed another CAB player and were very happy to enrol Jordanis Pavlides. I had looked on 'Pav' as a debonair man-about-town when I was a callow undergraduate, but he is still very much with us, the same trim figure, dividing the fairways at Ham Manor with well-directed, if foreshortened, blows.

With Yorkshire businessman Reg Corwen as non-playing captain, we had a very successful tournament at Montreux, not losing a single match. Meredith, as usual, was at the centre of the most amusing hand of the championship, though not in so heroic a role as in the last chapter.

South dealer
Love all

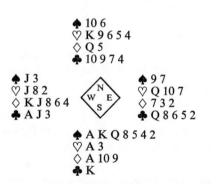

The Italian team contained such famous names as Belladonna, Forquet, Bianchi and Chiaradia, but at that time the Marmik pair, Franco and Giovine, had at least an equal reputation. Konstam and

Meredith had been making rings round them when the hand above was dealt. The bidding went:

South	West	North	East
Franco	Meredith	Giovine	Konstam
1 ◇	No	1 ♠	No
2 ♠	No	3 ♡	No
4 NT	No	5 ♣	No
6 ♠	No	No	No

Franco's 1 ◇ was the strong bid in the system and the response of 1 ♠ was point-showing (compare 1 ♡ over 1 ♣ in the Neapolitan).

Such an action would arouse no comment today, but Kempson waged a continual war against Marmik. How little he knew about it is shown by his comment in the *Bridge Magazine*: 'Giovine responded with a psychic (or perhaps semi-psychic) 1 ♠'.

At the end of the auction Meredith conducted his usual careful inquiry into all the bids—and then placed the ♠ J on the table! Giovine, the declarer, decided to accept the lead out of turn. This turned out to be a shrewd move, for he was able to get the heart suit going and draw the outstanding trumps with ♠ 10. The irony of the deal was that *no* lead from the East hand gives North any chance for the contract.

Despite this rather lucky swing to the Italians, we built up a good lead in the first half and held it in the second half. The final result at Montreux was Britain 26 victory points, France 23, Austria 22, Italy 19. In the match against Norway I played a hand in 4 ♠ with 9 8 6 of trumps in dummy, A 10 7 5 3 2 in hand. As there was a side loser I made the safety play of running the ♠ 6, which held the trick, West being void. I amused the kibitzers by remarking, 'It's a good thing I've read my book.' The Norwegian declarer at the other table evidently had not, for he failed in the contract.

In view of our handsome win at Montreux, it was resolved that the same team should represent Britain (and Europe) in the world championship to be played in New York early in 1955. Ellenby and Rosen, meanwhile, supported by Mathe, Moran and Bishop, had repeated, and even exceeded, their previous year's win in the Summer Nationals. They won all seven matches in the Round Robin. As a sixth player for the world championship, they chartered Alvin Roth.

Our hosts in New York were as hospitable as could be, but the match itself, played in a downstairs room at the Beekman Hotel, was not particularly well staged by modern standards and did not create much interest. Briefly, we took an early lead, lost it in the third quarter, went ahead strongly at the finish and won by 5,420 over 224 boards.

The final margin perhaps exaggerated our superiority. Even so, it has always been a slight mystery to me that after leading by 2,870 at the end of the first day we should have been a few points down at board 150. Man for man, I don't suppose there was much in it, but we had a big advantage in partnership experience. In general, there was a slightly disordered air about the American team. Their non-playing captain, Peter Leventritt, seldom arrived until he had completed his day's work at the Card School, and their partnerships were settled on a session-to-session basis. Roth, a brilliant player with an individual style, was not too easy to fit in. He and Ellenby played very well for a time, but this meant breaking up the Ellenby-Rosen partnership. Mathe and Moran, who played a bustling game very much in the British style, brought in most of the points when the Americans were fighting back.

British journalists, writing about the match, congratulated the British team on surviving the strain of the last two critical days. What strain? The programme was very light and it was not the first time any of us had been concerned in a tight match. The bridge writers also made much of Reg Corwen's captaincy, both on this and other occasions. I cannot say that he contributed much in a technical sense, but his straight-faced humour kept us in a good mood, which was important. Once, when I was playing golf with him at Juan-Les-Pins, his drive from the 11th tee nearly decapitated two players on an adjoining fairway. 'Sorry I was a bit slow in calling', said Reg when we caught up with them. 'I couldn't remember the French for Fore!'

Harold Franklin and I, working against time, produced a book of 100 selected hands from the world championship. This was published by De La Rue and very well presented, but like most books which are put out by a firm that does not specialize in the book trade, it had a disappointing circulation. For the lazy bridge public, if a book is not readily available in the shops, that's the end of it.

Is it possible to issue a suit-preference signal for the *trump* suit? There was certainly a case for it on this hand from the first day:

North dealer
Game all

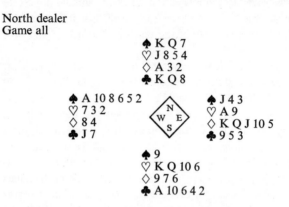

```
                    ♠ K Q 7
                    ♡ J 8 5 4
                    ◇ A 3 2
                    ♣ K Q 8
   ♠ A 10 8 6 5 2                   ♠ J 4 3
   ♡ 7 3 2              N           ♡ A 9
   ◇ 8 4            W     E         ◇ K Q J 10 5
   ♣ J 7               S            ♣ 9 5 3
                    ♠ 9
                    ♡ K Q 10 6
                    ◇ 9 7 6
                    ♣ A 10 6 4 2
```

The North hand was slightly below our standard for a vulnerable notrump, so Schapiro opened 1 ♣. Ellenby overcalled with 2 ◇. I could only say 3 ♣, and there we rested.

At the other table the bidding was:

South	West	North	East
Moran	Meredith	Mathe	Konstam
—	—	1 ♣	1 ◇
1 ♡	1 ♠	2 ♡	2 ♠
3 ♣	No	4 ♡	No
No	No		

Meredith led ◇ 8. Konstam held the first trick with the 10 and returned the jack, won in dummy. ♠ K went to the ace, and now West had to decide whether to try to put his partner in with a heart or a club. The best indication, it seemed to him, was his partner's lead of ◇ J, which perhaps was meant to suggest an entry in the lower-ranking suit. So Meredith led a club, which allowed South to dispose of his third diamond on ♠ Q and make the contract.

Perhaps this was not a good decision by Meredith, but the interesting point is that East could have dropped ♠ J when the king was led from dummy. As he had supported spades, this could only be a suit-preference signal for a trump switch.

On the third day, when our early lead was disappearing, Rosen and I both arrived at 6 ♣ on the following deal (switched to make South the declarer):

East dealer
Game all

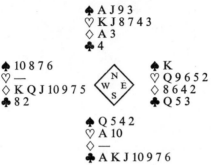

```
                    ♠ A J 9 3
                    ♡ K J 8 7 4 3
                    ◇ A 3
                    ♣ 4
    ♠ 10 8 7 6                         ♠ K
    ♡ —                                ♡ Q 9 6 5 2
    ◇ K Q J 10 9 7 5                   ◇ 8 6 4 2
    ♣ 8 2                              ♣ Q 5 3
                    ♠ Q 5 4 2
                    ♡ A 10
                    ◇ —
                    ♣ A K J 10 9 7 6
```

The bidding in Room 1:

South	West	North	East
Rosen	Pavlides	Ellenby	Meredith
—	—	—	No
1 ♣	3 ◇	3 ♡	4 ◇
6 ♣	No	No	No

South's 6 ♣ was an imaginative bid, based on two assumptions: that his partner's strength would not lie in diamonds and that even if there were two top losers in spades the suit might not be led.

The 6 ♣ bid was somewhat easier for me in Room 2:

South	West	North	East
Reese	Mathe	Schapiro	Moran
—	—	—	No
1 ♣	3 ◇	3 ♡	5 ◇
6 ♣	No	No	No

At both tables the ◇ 9 was led, containing a hint of the heart void. Rosen won with the ace, discarding a spade, and took the club finesse. When the clubs fell he lost only to ♠ K.

I followed a more complicated line, which was certain to win if ♣ Q came down in two rounds and would give me chances if East held ♣ Q x x. To preserve entries to dummy, I ruffed the diamond lead, cashed ♣ A and ♣ K, then played ♡ A and ♡ 10 to the

king. On the next trick East had to cover ♡ 7 with the 9. I ruffed
and exited with a trump, leaving East to play in this position:

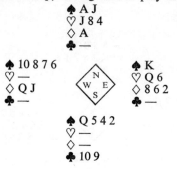

      ♠ A J
      ♡ J 8 4
      ◇ A
      ♣ —

♠ 10 8 7 6   ♠ K
♡ —   ♡ Q 6
◇ Q J   ◇ 8 6 2
♣ —   ♣ —

      ♠ Q 5 4 2
      ♡ —
      ◇ —
      ♣ 10 9

If East plays a heart or a diamond now, I can establish two tricks in
hearts. He took his best chance by advancing ♠ K.

Finally, there was a simple but instructive point on this hand,
which ended the fifth day:

East dealer
E-W vulnerable

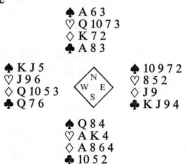

      ♠ A 6 3
      ♡ Q 10 7 3
      ◇ K 7 2
      ♣ A 8 3

♠ K J 5   ♠ 10 9 7 2
♡ J 9 6   ♡ 8 5 2
◇ Q 10 5 3   ◇ J 9
♣ Q 7 6   ♣ K J 9 4

      ♠ Q 8 4
      ♡ A K 4
      ◇ A 8 6 4
      ♣ 10 5 2

Konstam played 3 NT from the North position and had no chance
after the lead of the ♠ 10. We had to work a little harder at my
table, where the bidding went:

South	West	North	East
Bishop	Schapiro	Mathe	Reese
—	—	—	No
1 ◇	No	1 ♡	No
1 NT	No	3 NT	No
No	No		

As diamonds and hearts had been called against him, West led ♣ 6 and dummy played low. I could tell that ♣ 6 was not fourth best, so I put in the *jack* and switched to ♠ 10. Declarer can make the contract if he does everything right—let ♠ 10 run to the ace and take four rounds of hearts, putting West to an awkward discard. However, the winning line is far from clear and in practice I came in again with ♣ K to lead a second spade. Note that the play of ♣ J at trick one does not cost a trick even if declarer holds the queen. If East wins the first trick with ♣ K and continues the suit, South will probably hold up until the third round, take four rounds of hearts, and end-play West in diamonds and spades.

After the match in New York we went to Florida, where we were accommodated in great style at one of the big hotels in Miami. Boris was unable to make the trip and my recollection is that Dodds was able to play on only one day, so our team for the most part was Konstam and Pavlides, Meredith and myself. Our opponents included such stars as Charles Goren, Bill Root, Harold Harkavy, von Zedtwitz and Billy Seamon. There was never much in it and we lost eventually by 150 aggregate points. I remember with annoyance that on the last hand I made a mistake which may be said to have cost the match. It was one of those hands where the declarer needs to go to and fro in the trump suit to establish dummy's long suit and an early trump lead will inconvenience him. I don't recall the exact deal, only that the contract was 5 ♣. The theme is illustrated in this deal:

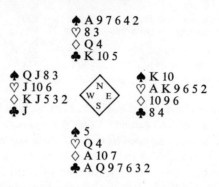

```
                    ♠ A 9 7 6 4 2
                    ♡ 8 3
                    ♢ Q 4
                    ♣ K 10 5

    ♠ Q J 8 3                       ♠ K 10
    ♡ J 10 6          N             ♡ A K 9 6 5 2
    ♢ K J 5 3 2    W     E          ♢ 10 9 6
    ♣ J              S              ♣ 8 4

                    ♠ 5
                    ♡ Q 4
                    ♢ A 10 7
                    ♣ A Q 9 7 6 3 2
```

South is in 5 ♣ and the defence begins with two rounds of hearts. It looks fairly natural for East to play a diamond next, but South goes up with the ace, takes a spade ruff and uses the three trump entries to set up two long spades. The diamond play by East really has no meaning, for if West has ◊ A it won't run away. It is essential to lead a trump before declarer can use the entry to dummy as part of his plan to establish the spades.

eleven

NOT WITH SEEMLINESS

In the middle of 1954 the B.B.L. announced that the winners of the Gold Cup would be invited to consider themselves the Probable team for the European Championship at Amsterdam in 1955. As the winners were unable to accept, the runners-up, Joel Tarlo's team, became the Probables, open to challenge by the team that held the European and world championships. Moreover, the Probables were accorded a tactical advantage, to the extent that if they lost the first match they would have the right to play a further 100 boards.

There was some criticism of this arrangement, naturally, but the B.B.L. had to stand by the scheme it had announced and I did not take the view, then or now, that any team should represent the country just on past achievement. Trials should be held and at the end of them the selectors should make their decision, taking past and present form into consideration.

On the present occasion Joel Tarlo waived his right to any advantage. It was agreed that the match should be extended to 150 boards if the margin at the end of 100 were less than 10 I.M.P.s to either side.

We gained a rather lucky slam swing on the first board, and this was Board 2:

East dealer
N-S vulnerable

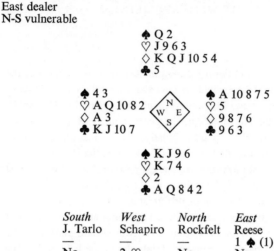

```
                    ♠ Q 2
                    ♡ J 9 6 3
                    ◇ K Q J 10 5 4
                    ♣ 5
    ♠ 4 3                         ♠ A 10 8 7 5
    ♡ A Q 10 8 2      N           ♡ 5
    ◇ A 3          W     E        ◇ 9 8 7 6
    ♣ K J 10 7        S           ♣ 9 6 3
                    ♠ K J 9 6
                    ♡ K 7 4
                    ◇ 2
                    ♣ A Q 8 4 2
```

South	West	North	East
J. Tarlo	Schapiro	Rockfelt	Reese
—	—	—	1 ♠ (1)
No	2 ♡	No	No
2 NT (2)	No	3 ◇	No
3 NT (3)	Dble	Redble	No
No	No		

(1) As Meredith was absent in the South of France, I decided to fill the gap with one of his typical psychic bids in the spade suit.

(2) When East passes 2 ♡ everyone knows that the opening bid was psychic. It is still difficult for North-South to achieve any rapport. An optional double would have turned out well.

(3) This looks rash, but you can see what was going through his mind: 'I hold the spades well, perhaps partner will have a bolster in clubs . . .'

West led a low heart, won by dummy's 9. On ◇ K I played the 8, indicating an even number, so West knew there could be no point in holding up the ace. (In this type of situation declarer should normally aim to make the first lead through the defender who is likely to hold the ace, before this player has had the chance to see a card from his partner.) Ace and another heart left South in the lead, and when ♠ Q lost to the ace declarer could make only six tricks, conceding a penalty of 1,000.

The match became quite close near the finish, but we won without needing to play the extra boards. In the end I didn't go to Amsterdam because towards the end of the year I had a minor operation.

Meredith and Joel Tarlo were drafted, but the partnerships did not seem to settle down and the team finished seventh.

In January 1956 the *British Bridge World* was revived for the first time since the war, taking over from the *Contract Bridge Journal*. The *British Bridge World* was published by De La Rue and I was editor for the next seven years. We had a very strong team from the first. Harrison-Gray wrote a series of 'Famous Hands from Famous Matches', Alan Truscott presented 'Hands of the Month', Alfred Sheinwold sent us the news from America, Jean Besse from Switzerland.

Hubert Phillips, who was on the editorial board, started a feature called 'What They Say About Bridge'. In the second issue we achieved a notable *coup* in the form of an article specially written by Somerset Maugham. I think it was Konstam who organized this; he had played with Maugham in the South of France and in London. Here is an extract:

Bridge is the most diverting and intelligent card game that the wit of man has so far devised. I would have children taught it as a matter of course, just as they are taught dancing; in the end it will be more useful to them, for you cannot with seemliness continue to dance when you are bald and potbellied; nor, for that matter, can you with satisfaction to yourself or pleasure to your partner continue to play tennis or golf when you are well past middle age. But you can play bridge so long as you can sit up at a table and tell one card from another. In fact, when all else fails—sport, love, ambition —bridge remains a solace and an entertainment.

It is hard to reward the famous, but De La Rue had the happy idea of sending Mr Maugham 12 packs of cards with his photograph on the ace of spades. I was reminded of Henry Riddell's embarrassment when Ely Culbertson made a guest appearance in 'Bridge on the Air'. 'I handed him a cheque for 15 guineas and disappeared before he could open the envelope.'

My first assignment for the *British Bridge World* was to cover the 1956 world championship between France, the winners at Amsterdam, and America. The teams were:

France: Jais and Trézel, Ghestem and Bacherich, Romanet and Lattès; non-playing captain, Baron de Nexon.

America: Stayman, Solomon, Kahn, Field, Hazen, Goren; the first five had won the American team championship and Goren was added as sixth man; non-playing captain, Jeff Glick.

Note that I name the French team in pairs; the Americans interchanged partnerships.

When I arrived at the match on the afternoon of the second day, the fog that had delayed my journey had settled low over the American players. The USA had led by 18 points at the first interval on Sunday, but now Stayman and Solomon were having a rough time against Jais and Trézel in the open room. They missed two slams and then came a hand that showed which way the wind was likely to blow for the rest of the match:

East dealer
Game all

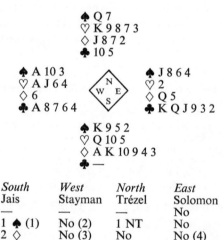

♠ Q 7
♥ K 9 8 7 3
♦ J 8 7 2
♣ 10 5

♠ A 10 3
♥ A J 6 4
♦ 6
♣ A 8 7 6 4

♠ J 8 6 4
♥ 2
♦ Q 5
♣ K Q J 9 3 2

♠ K 9 5 2
♥ Q 10 5
♦ A K 10 9 4 3
♣ —

South	West	North	East
Jais	Stayman	Trézel	Solomon
—	—	—	No
1 ♠ (1)	No (2)	1 NT	No
2 ♦	No (3)	No	No (4)

(1) This pair played the *canapé* style, in which it is normal to bid the shorter suit first.

(2) West has no satisfactory overcall at this point.

(3) Now Sam Stayman missed a chance to double, showing values in the unbid suits.

(4) Surely East should reopen with 3 ♣? His opponents have followed a limited sequence and West must hold some values.

Eleven tricks were made for a score of 150 to North-South. At the other table Ghestem opened 3 ♣ as East, South doubled for take-out and the final contract was 5 ♣, doubled by North. A diamond was led, followed by a heart switch. At an early stage Ghestem led ♠ J, covered by the king and ace. After the red suits had been eliminated a second spade was won by North, who had to concede a ruff-and-discard.

France won the match by 54 match points. (This was the old scale; the margin under the present scale would have been greater, about 80.) The Americans gained on three of the six days and on 11 out of 20 sessions, but they played poorly on two days, and the French never lost their rhythm.

At the banquet after the match an official voice announced: 'Full records of the world championship match are on sale at the door. To buy them costs 1,000 francs.' Voice from Charles Goren: 'What does it cost to destroy them?'

Jimmy Ortiz-Patino had much success in Paris with a story arising from the fact that the American Ambassador, Mr Douglas Dillon, was *Président d'honneur* of the organizing committee. When the ambassador's wife held her regular bridge tea-party the following week, she surprised her friends by raising her cards above her head and waving them to and fro in the direction of the unseeing walls behind. Asked to explain this strange conduct, she said: 'My husband was watching the international players last week and, he says they did this before every hand.'

Like their predecessors the year before, the American team came to London after playing in Paris. The match was played at Selfridges, with a display board and a fishbowl (a glass-fronted panel in which the players were visible to the audience). The home team was the same quintet as before—Konstam, Dodds, Mayer, Schapiro, Reese —and the story of the match was the same too, a heavy defeat for the visitors. The Americans sustained a nasty blow early on:

South dealer
N-S vulnerable

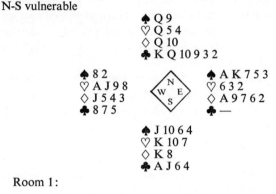

```
                          ♠ Q 9
                          ♡ Q 5 4
                          ◇ Q 10
                          ♣ K Q 10 9 3 2
        ♠ 8 2                              ♠ A K 7 5 3
        ♡ A J 9 8          N               ♡ 6 3 2
        ◇ J 5 4 3      W        E          ◇ A 9 7 6 2
        ♣ 8 7 5            S               ♣ —
                          ♠ J 10 6 4
                          ♡ K 10 7
                          ◇ K 8
                          ♣ A J 6 4
```

Room 1:

South	West	North	East
Dodds	Solomon	Konstam	Hazen
1 ♣	No	3 ♣	Dble
No	3 ♡	3 NT	No
No	No		

East's lead of a low spade ran to the declarer's queen, and at trick 2 Konstam led a heart to the king and ace. At this point a spade to the king and a heart from East leaves the declarer a trick short, but this defence was not easy to find and in practice Solomon returned a heart, which Konstam ran to the 10. That was 600 to North-South. As Truscott remarked in his commentary, Lee Hazen might have considered leading ♠ K instead of a low one; then a view of the dummy would have suggested a diamond switch.

In Room 2:

South	West	North	East
Field	Reese	Stayman	Schapiro
No	No	1 ♣	1 ♠
2 NT	No	No	3 ◇
No	No	3 NT	No
No	4 ◇	No	No
Dble	No	No	No

Most players, no doubt, would have doubled 4 ◇, as Myron Field did, but a close examination of the bidding would have revealed some warning signs. Partner's 3 NT was probably based on a club suit, so ♣ A might not live. Diamonds were quite likely to be

5-4-2-2 round the table. So, was there any certainty of four defensive tricks? Perhaps one should say that it would have been a very fine decision *not* to double. Schapiro made ten tricks and, on the surface, might have made eleven; anyway, it was a further 510 to the home side.

The Americans found their best form in the third match of their tour, scoring a big victory against the Swiss team. I recall that most players in Britain, still more in America, no doubt, were surprised at France's win in the world championship. Looking back, one can see that the Americans had no partnerships as solid as Jais and Trézel, Ghestem and Bacherich. I have always blamed myself for not making one or two shrewd investments on the outcome.

twelve

COLLISION COURSE

If you would like to plunge into the whirlpool that caused great disturbance at Stockholm in 1956, consider the following hand, held by South:

♠ 10 9 7   ♡ A 8 4 3 2   ◇ K 10 6   ♣ 9 5

At love all North, your partner, opens 1 ♣. You respond 1 ♡ and West comes in with 1 ♠. Partner forces with 3 ◇, you rebid 3 ♡ and partner leaps to 6 ♡. At this point East enters with a sacrifice of 6 ♠. The bidding so far:

South	West	North	East
—	—	1 ♣	No
1 ♡	1 ♠	3 ◇	No
3 ♡	No	6 ♡	6 ♠
?			

Now, if you want to join in the game, formulate your answers to the following questions:

1. What action do you take over 6 ♠?

This is not the critical question. In practice South passed, which in itself is understandable. His partner considered for a long while, then doubled. These two questions then arise:

2. In a purely technical sense, what would you call now?

3. Supposing that your judgement told you that you ought to bid 7 ♡, would you, on a point of ethics, consider that you were inhibited from doing so because your partner had pondered before doubling 6 ♠? (The point being, of course, that partner must have contemplated bidding 7 ♡ himself.)

The situation arose in the match between Britain and Switzerland. I was not directly involved because, as will appear below, my role this year was to captain the British ladies. This was the full deal that led to the protest:

North dealer
Love all

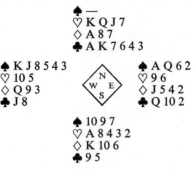

```
                    ♠ —
                    ♡ K Q J 7
                    ◇ A 8 7
                    ♣ A K 7 6 4 3
♠ K J 8 5 4 3                        ♠ A Q 6 2
♡ 10 5              N                ♡ 9 6
◇ Q 9 3          W     E             ◇ J 5 4 2
♣ J 8              S                 ♣ Q 10 2
                    ♠ 10 9 7
                    ♡ A 8 4 3 2
                    ◇ K 10 6
                    ♣ 9 5
```

The bidding in the open room went:

South	West	North	East
Besse	Franklin	Ortiz	L. Tarlo
—	—	1 ♣	No
1 ♡	1 ♠	3 ◇	No
3 ♡	No	6 ♡	6 ♠
No	No	Dble	No
7 ♡	No	No	No

It was not disputed that there had been a pause before North's double of 6 ♠ and also before South's bid of 7 ♡.

As soon as Besse bid 7 ♡, West called for the tournament director, saying that he wished to reserve his rights. The grand slam was made and the tournament director accepted Besse's explanation of why he bid it. The British took the matter to the Appeals Committee, which upheld the director's ruling but to some extent spoiled the effect by issuing some general warnings 'especially to the Swiss'.

Meanwhile, the *Bulletin* had given much publicity to the affair, allowing the protagonists to have their say while the matter was still *sub judice*. Besse contended that his holding of an ace and a king justified his bid of 7 ♡ and that his partner's hesitation before doubling meant absolutely nothing. Nobody, least of all Jimmy, would make a hurried decision in such a dramatic situation. The British accepted that South might reasonably pass over 6 ♠. They felt, however, that North's hesitation before doubling 6 ♠ must have resolved certain doubts, in particular about the quality of his trump support. In such cases the test to apply, according to tournament regulations, is not whether the player *was* influenced but whether any sensible player would have taken the same action (i.e., have bid 7 ♡) irrespective of the hesitation.

These matters are very hard to determine and people tend to take sides quite unreasonably. On the present occasion a Scandinavian journalist expressed the most exaggerated views, declaring that Besse had used tactics that were 'strictly against the spirit of the Laws of Bridge'. Such impertinence, after the tournament director, and later the Appeals Committee, had accepted the player's explanation!

There was a remarkably close echo of this affair during the 1976 Bermuda Bowl final at Monte Carlo. Hamilton and Eisenberg, for the USA, held these cards:

West	East
♠ A 2	♠ K 8 6
♡ K Q J	♡ A 9 8 6 5 4 2
◇ A K J 7	◇ Q 4
♣ A 8 7 5	♣ 10

With neither side vulnerable the bidding went:

South Forquet	West Hamilton	North Belladonna	East Eisenberg
—	—	No	3 ♡
No	4 NT	No	5 ◇
No	5 NT	No	6 ◇
No	6 ♡	No	7 ♡
No	No	No	

Here, too, West thought long before deciding to bid only 6 ♡. The Italians protested on the grounds that East, who had already shown his ace and king by the responses to Blackwood, had no right to bid 7 ♡ after his partner had tranced before settling for 6 ♡. (This last bid, by the way, was distinctly on the nervous side: West could count 12 top tricks after his partner had shown an ace and a king.)

Eisenberg's answer was that he had a maximum pre-empt by American standards; true, he had shown the ace and king, but his shape was 7-3-2-1, not the more sterile 7-2-2-2, and ◇ Q was an important extra value. His partner must be interested in a grand slam because he had bid 5 NT over 5 ◇.

The tournament director accepted Eisenberg's explanation; so

did the Appeals Committee, by a narrow majority, and the full
Executive Committee by a wider margin.

Some people thought the Americans had been a little lucky to
survive the protest. How could East be sure the trumps were solid,
they asked. Here they missed a technical point: if West's trumps had
been no better than K x or Q J x x he would not have asked for
kings over 5 ◊ but would have bid a new suit, directing partner's
attention to the quality of his trumps.

To complete the story of these two deals, the British pair at the
other table in the Britain-Switzerland match stopped in 6 ♡, and in
the Bermuda Bowl Garozzo and Franco bid the grand slam after
East had opened with a weak 2 ♡.

As I said above, I was not in the British team this year. There had
been the usual commotion over the trials. After the moderate showing at Amsterdam the B.B.L. adopted a new scheme, designed, it was
said, to give players the experience of playing in different formations
and so to establish mutual confidence. Fourteen players were invited to join a panel from which the team from Stockholm would be
selected. The players were told that they would be required to meet
for practice once a month and to play as B.B.L. nominees in a
number of events.

This was something quite new. My own view was that players had
a right to make up their own teams for national events; that the
practices would achieve nothing and that the whole scheme was
unrealistic in its professed object of improving Britain's chances in
the European Championship.

Four leading players—Konstam, Dodds, Schapiro and myself—
declined to take part in the panel scheme but declared themselves
willing to play in any trials that would help the selectors to find the
best team. Two other players who could not spare the time to take
part in the scheme also withdrew, so the panel was reduced to eight.

It has always been my experience that the obstinacy of individuals
increases in geometrical progression when they are associated as
members of an official body, and the B.B.L. showed no sign of
modifying its plans. There were two ways of regarding the general
situation and Guy Ramsey posed the alternatives in a letter to the
Daily Telegraph:

Are these four players a collection of *prima donnas* . . . so confident of their own prowess that they are insubordinate to the discipline necessarily exerted by the governing body of the game? Or are the B.B.L. and their selectors more sensible of their own dignity and the sacrosanctity of their plans than they are concerned to find the best possible team?

Of course, it is wrong for players to seek to coerce the governing body. We were not doing that, however; we were simply saying that if these were the conditions we were content to give the championship a miss.

While the arguments were going on, my team and the B.B.L. panel team were pursuing what the dramatic writers call a collision course in the Gold Cup, and we did indeed meet in the final. Boris and I played below form on the first day, but we won comfortably enough in the end by 46 (old) I.M.P. The panel team did well at Stockholm, however, losing to none of the teams in the lower half and finishing fourth in a year when Italy and France werè both very strongly represented.

As I was on the sidelines I was offered (as consolation or penalty?) the captaincy of the ladies' team, which consisted of Mrs Markus, Mrs Gordon, Miss Shanahan, Mrs Lester, Mrs Williams and Mrs van Rees (now Marjorie Hiron). Mrs Markus and Mrs Gordon did not have one of their best championships and the team finished fifth. France won very narrowly from Belgium, with Sweden third and Norway fourth.

My captaincy was successful in one respect: there were no cross words, no recriminations within the team, despite the disappointing progress. It was left to the partisans, on our return home, to introduce a note of discord. Meredith and Juan thought that some of the press reports made too much of Dorothy Shanahan's good play. In an article entitled 'Pride—and Prejudice' they referred to a column in 'an agricultural magazine' (Gray in *Country Life*!) and to Truscott's report in the *British Bridge World*, which spoke of the high standard of play in a match that was narrowly lost. Examining some hands from the first half of this match, they professed to discover 27 I.M.P. thrown away at Dorothy's table. Maintaining the Jane Austen style, Gray, in 'Sense—and Sensibility', Truscott in 'Females—and Fallibility', rushed to the defence, exhibiting their own brand of 'Persuasion'.

That Pedro Juan should have been one of the authors of the article that led to the correspondence was mildly ironical, for there was no more partial supporter than himself. I remember when his romance with the former Jane Garratt was in its early stages. 'Mark my words, Terree,' he said, wagging his finger at me. 'Mark my words, Terree, my little Jane will play for England one day.'

All Pedro's geese were swans in his eyes, but this time he was right. Jane not only played several times for Britain but as Jane Juan she won two world championships. Since then, of course, she has won many big events with her present husband, Tony Priday.

thirteen

A BIG BUILD-UP

For its Christmas Competition at the end of 1955 the *Observer* invited readers to parody any of the paper's regular features. This parody of the bridge article won a prize for Mr Stanley Norman, of Montevideo:

BRIDGE
by Terence Reese

The Outer Mongolian Bridge team, at present touring Britain, has aroused considerable interest and speculation here. The Mongolians are astute and resourceful players, who have introduced one or two novel and spectacular conventions, particularly the psychic pre-emptive bid and psychic pass. That these can sometimes be double-edged weapons is demonstrated on the following hand from their match against the Crampton Ladies' Social Club:

```
            Dealer, South    Game all
                 ♠ 10 9 8
                 ♡ J 10 9
                 ♢ J 10 9
                 ♣ J 10 9 8
   ♠ 5 4 3                      ♠ 7 6 2
   ♡ 5 4 3 2        N           ♡ 8 7 6
   ♢ 5 4 3      W     E         ♢ 8 7 6 2
   ♣ 5 4 3         S            ♣ 7 6 2
                 ♠ A K Q J
                 ♡ A K Q
                 ♢ A K Q
                 ♣ A K Q
```

This was the bidding in Room 1, where the Mongolians were East-West:

South	West	North	East
Mrs	Tsao	Miss	Tse-Tse
Prook	Chin	Gepp	Klun
2 ♣	5 ♠ (!)	No	No
Dble	No	No	5 NT (!!)
Dble	No	No	No

West's bid of Five Spades was a gallant, but misguided, attempt to prevent opponents from reaching what he rightly regarded as a certain slam. When Klun unwisely rescued into notrumps, Mrs Prook had no hesitation in doubling.

In Room 2 the Mongolian South unfortunately tried a psychic No Bid and the hand was passed out. The net result was a heavy swing in favour of the ladies.

The sentence, in particular, beginning 'That these can sometimes be double-edged weapons . . .' was a brilliant parody of my style.

To captain the British ladies, like execution on the block, is an ordeal one is not asked to undergo twice, and I was a candidate for the open team at Vienna in 1957. After two stages of team trials my team was scheduled to play five matches of 32 boards against Preston's team. We were a little ahead after four matches, but one of our players was unable to take part in the last match and the B.B.L. refused to allow a substitute, because the trials this year were supposed to be a test of stamina, reflecting conditions in the championship itself. In the end some sort of amalgamation took place and a strong team went to Vienna—Rose, Gardener, Konstam, Meredith, Schapiro, Reese. The team played well, losing no matches, but we had six draws and finished only third to Italy and Austria. This amusing episode was from our match against Iceland:

West dealer
Game all

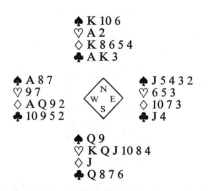

```
                    ♠ K 10 6
                    ♡ A 2
                    ◇ K 8 6 5 4
                    ♣ A K 3
   ♠ A 8 7                        ♠ J 5 4 3 2
   ♡ 9 7             N            ♡ 6 5 3
   ◇ A Q 9 2      W     E         ◇ 10 7 3
   ♣ 10 9 5 2        S            ♣ J 4
                    ♠ Q 9
                    ♡ K Q J 10 8 4
                    ◇ J
                    ♣ Q 8 7 6
```

After a pass by West I opened 1 NT in the North position. East passed, and Schapiro bid 4 ♡.

End of bidding, do you think? Well, no, because we were playing the old form of Texas, whereby 4 ◇ was a transfer to 4 ♡ and 4 ♡ a transfer to 4 ♠. Moreover, we had agreed that anyone who forgot the convention should pay a fine of 100 Austrian schillings. So, over 4 ♡ I transferred to 4 ♠. At this point 5 ♡ by South might sound like a slam try in spades, so Schapiro bid 6 ♡, to enlighten me. The

Icelander on lead, having missed the by-play, opened with ♠ A—and followed with another spade, thinking that South must be void of diamonds. The singleton diamond now went away on ♠ K and West was later squeezed in the minor suits.

After this little incident the rest of the team insisted that we should play 'South African Texas', whereby 4 ♣ asks for 4 ♡, 4 ◇ for 4 ♠ —an arrangement that is easier to remember. I said, 'No, make the penalty 200 schillings.'

There have been other instances of a very lucky result arising from a misunderstanding. The following occurred when a Finnish pair held the North-South cards in a match between Helsinki and Stockholm:

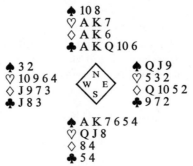

```
            ♠ 10 8
            ♡ A K 7
            ◇ A K 6
            ♣ A K Q 10 6
♠ 3 2                        ♠ Q J 9
♡ 10 9 6 4      N            ♡ 5 3 2
◇ J 9 7 3    W     E         ◇ Q 10 5 2
♣ J 8 3         S            ♣ 9 7 2
            ♠ A K 7 6 5 4
            ♡ Q J 8
            ◇ 8 4
            ♣ 5 4
```

North opened with a conventional 2 ♣ and the bidding proceeded as follows:

South	North
—	2 ♣
2 ♡ (1)	2 NT
4 ♡ (2)	7 ♡ (3)
No (4)	

(1) A conventional reply, denoting an ace and a king.

(2) Transfer bids over notrumps were played elsewhere in the system, and South intended here to show a six-card suit of spades.

(3) Either forgetting the system or thinking that transfers would not be used in this sequence.

(4) He knows there has been a misunderstanding but decides to take his chance in hearts; partner might hold A K 10 x and 7 ♡ be a better contract than 7 ♠.

West led ♠ 3 and declarer made the first eight tricks by way of seven winners in the side suits and a diamond ruff in hand. West was down to ♡ 10 9 6 4 and ◇ J, but his trumps were caught in the diagonal crossfire. On the next spade he went in with ♡ 9; dummy overruffed and South made the rest of the tricks on a crossruff.

The firm of De La Rue celebrated its 60th anniversary in 1957 and two very successful promotions were held at Selfridges. The first was a five-session pairs contest in which 26 pairs from 24 countries took part. This marked the first appearance in Britain of the famed partnership of Charles Goren and Helen Sobel, who upheld their reputation by winning the event. The holders of the American Masters Pairs, Sanborn Brown and Martin Cohn, were runners-up.

The pairs tournament was followed by a Par Contest, for which the hands were set by Harold Franklin and myself. In this, the best overall score was recorded by Rose and Squire, playing North-South, while Bourchtoff and Svarc of France, MacLaren and Forbes of Scotland, headed the East-West side. There were several difficult hands, but none that defeated every competitor. Dr Forbes was the only player to survive the following test:

South dealer
N-S vulnerable

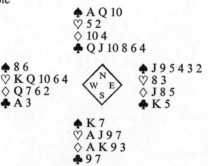

```
                    ♠ A Q 10
                    ♡ 5 2
                    ◇ 10 4
                    ♣ Q J 10 8 6 4
    ♠ 8 6                          ♠ J 9 5 4 3 2
    ♡ K Q 10 6 4       N           ♡ 8 3
    ◇ Q 7 6 2      W       E       ◇ J 8 5
    ♣ A 3              S           ♣ K 5
                    ♠ K 7
                    ♡ A J 9 7
                    ◇ A K 9 3
                    ♣ 9 7
```

In a par contest you have a directed contract and a directed lead. Before the play begins, a slip containing the suggested bidding is studied by all the players. In this case the suggested bidding was:

South	West	North	East
1 ♡	No	2 ♣	No
2 ◇	No	2 NT	No
3 NT	Dble	No	No
No			

North-South scored their par for reaching 3 NT, but there was no bidding par for East-West. East scored the 'lead par' for opening ♡ 8 in response to his partner's double.

The ♡ 8 is covered by the 9 and 10, and at trick 2 . . .

Caught you! West must *not* cover the ♡ 9 with the 10. His only hope is that his partner can win the first round of clubs and lead a second heart while West still has an entry card. It is a standard ducking play, really, but difficult to recognize in this setting.

This was one of the more spectacular hands:

South dealer
Game all

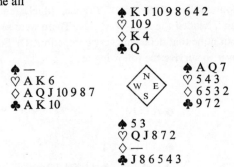

```
                    ♠ K J 10 9 8 6 4 2
                    ♡ 10 9
                    ◇ K 4
                    ♣ Q
 ♠ —                              ♠ A Q 7
 ♡ A K 6              N            ♡ 5 4 3
 ◇ A Q J 10 9 8 7   W   E          ◇ 6 5 3 2
 ♣ A K 10             S            ♣ 9 7 2
                    ♠ 5 3
                    ♡ Q J 8 7 2
                    ◇ —
                    ♣ J 8 6 5 4 3
```

The suggested bidding was:

South	West	North	East
No	2 ♣	3 ♠	3NT
No	6 ◇	No	No
No			

North-South scored their par for bidding 3 ♠ or 4 ♠ on the first round and making no further bid. East-West scored full points for a final bid of 5 ◇ or 6 ◇, or a game bid in notrumps, or a double of 5 ♠ or higher.

North leads ♡ 10 against 6 ◇, and at trick two West lays down ◇ A. To quote from the official analysis:

If North is alert he will observe that dummy has no entry in the trump suit. To have any hope of defeating the contract, North must assume that West is void in spades. There is an obvious danger, however, that after one round of trumps West will cash winners in hearts and clubs and then put North in with ◇ K, forcing him to lead into dummy's spades. Thus the right defence is to throw ◇ K under the ace hoping that West will have two losers.

West can still make the contract, however. On the first round of clubs North drops the queen. This can be read as a singleton, both because false-carding is disallowed in the contest and because with ♣ Q J and a singleton heart the club would have been a better opening lead. After two rounds of trumps and one of clubs West throws the lead to South in hearts, forcing him to play into the club tenace.

North-South scored their playing par for dropping ◇ K under the ace, and East-West for making twelve tricks whatever the defence.

I was doing the commentary for 300 spectators in the Exhibition Hall at Selfridges and the North-South pair in the fishbowl, as it happened, was Sobel and Goren. Naturally I gave the situation a big build-up. Could she, would she . . . ? And then, when ◇ A was led, Helen Sobel dropped the king as though it were the card nearest her thumb! Of course, there was drama in that, too. The play was made at four tables out of twelve.

My favourite hand from the contest was the following, because it involved no recognized form of technique, just unusual perception:

West dealer
E-W vulnerable

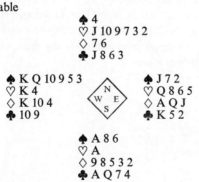

```
                ♠ 4
                ♡ J 10 9 7 3 2
                ◇ 7 6
                ♣ J 8 6 3

♠ K Q 10 9 5 3              ♠ J 7 2
♡ K 4            N          ♡ Q 8 6 5
◇ K 10 4      W   E         ◇ A Q J
♣ 10 9            S         ♣ K 5 2

                ♠ A 8 6
                ♡ A
                ◇ 9 8 5 3 2
                ♣ A Q 7 4
```

East-West scored their par for reaching 4 ♠, with consolation for 3 ♠.

A club lead would beat the contract at once, but the normal, and directed, lead was ♡ J. South wins with ♡ A and can see promise of three defensive tricks—but will he live to enjoy ♣ Q as well? West (who has rebid his spades) is sure to have five tricks in spades, two in hearts, and three in diamonds—if given time to make them.

There is only one chance—that North has ♣ J. At trick two South returns ♣ Q, tunnelling a way into his partner's hand. Winning the first or second round of spades, South plays a low club to his partner's jack and ruffs a heart to defeat the contract.

Some competitors (Goren among them) tried a low club at trick two—not quite good enough, because West's 9 forces the jack and there is then no entry to the North hand. The correct defence was found by Heidenfeld (South Africa), Yallouze (Egypt), Savostin (Belgium), Reithtoffer (Austria), Kock (Sweden) and D'Alelio (Italy). The rest must have kicked themselves for missing it—and that is the test of a good par hand.

After our exertions in promoting and directing the two events at Selfridges, Harold Franklin and I visited Porthcawl for the Congress in November. During one of our needle matches on the golf course, Harold played a good second shot to the edge of the third green. As he crested the brow of the fairway he was dismayed to see a black bird rolling his ball along with its beak. As he drew nearer, the bird, alarmed by the conflicting advice of player and opponent, picked up the ball and took to flight. Harold pursued it with hoarse cries, brandishing his club, scaled a boundary wall and disappeared into a meadow, his green cap bobbing in the mist, while the bird wheeled superciliously aloft.

fourteen

A STRONG APPLAUD

During the 1950s I wrote one or two articles on Bridgemanship, a subject to which I have given some thought. The word stands for a combination of Gamesmanship and One-Upmanship, made famous by Stephen Potter.

Gamesmanship is the art of gaining an advantage without doing anything unfair. One-Upmanship is the art of establishing your superiority in an inconspicuous way. Dramatic critics are practised exponents. 'The [tiny] part of so-and-so has not been so well realized since Gielgud's production in . . .'

Bridge, to be sure, was not overlooked by Potter himself. The ploys and gambits which are the life-work of a professional player are wittily reflected in the conversations that attend the preliminaries to a friendly rubber.

(There, in case you have missed the point, is an inartistic essay in One-Upmanship. The impression is left that Potter's treatment of Bridgemanship was on the tea-party level—unspecialized, derivative, lacking insight into the arcana of the tournament world.)

The preliminaries attending the choice of seats in a team-of-four match provide an early opportunity. Let us say that your opponents have to seat first. Choosing their strongest formation, they grimly take their places.

Now you hold a parley among the five or six members of your team. The waiting opponents hear snatches of conversation such as: 'Who feels like starting?' . . . 'Can I come in after 8 boards, I want to watch the racing' . . . 'Better not rely on me, I was playing back-gammon till 4 o'clock this morning.'

Finally, you take your seats in the formation which you had always intended. Then comes the exchange of system information. The opponents draw your attention to the card that sets out their methods. You examine this with unseeing eyes, nod sagely, and say, 'Sort of Precision, eh?' or, if it *is* Precision, 'Sort of Blue Club?'

'What about you?' they ask. 'Oh, nothing special. We'll tap if there's anything you might not understand.'

There is no need to score. After five or six hands you say: 'Are you keeping score, partner?'

'No, I thought you were.'

'One of us had better. Give me a score-card, I'll copy them down.'

'You can do it at half-time.'

By now, the opponents will be almost ashamed to *try*. You are One Up.

At half-time assure the pair at your table that they have done well. Make a lot of some hand on which the result obtained by your side is superficially bad but will probably be the same at the other table. If possible, repeat this judgement in the hearing of the other pair ('Your boys have been too good for us'). This will put them on the defensive if their team is not ahead.

Most players have some idiosyncrasies or foibles which are worth noting. One quite well-known player is put completely out of temper if someone borrows his pencil and will not continue the game until it is restored.

How do I know?

Try borrowing mine!

Early in 1958 we had some fun with Guy Ramsey's answer to one of his problems in the *Daily Telegraph* Christmas Competition. It read:

6. (a) 2 NT—5 marks; 6 NT—4; 7 NT—2; No Bid—1.

Obviously a view.*

The Italian team that had won at Stockholm in 1956 beat the United States by over 10,000 points in New York the following January. The Americans were still keeping to their policy of choosing the winners of the Summer Nationals, and the teams that had lost in turn to Britain, France and Italy were not in every respect the strongest that could have been chosen. In 1957, however, they had more luck, if you can call it luck: the winners were Crawford, Becker, Rapee and Silodor, and for the world championship they

---

* It would not be fair to Guy Ramsey (or to present readers) to leave it like that. As Guy explained in a subsequent issue of the *British Bridge World*, the situation was that South had opened 1 NT not vulnerable, West had doubled, and East, vulnerable with about 19 points, and playing in a pairs, had a problem which could be resolved in a number of ways.

added Roth and Stone. Except, perhaps, that Schenken would always have been worth his place, this was a truly representative team. Thus the clash with Italy at Lake Como in January 1958 was eagerly awaited. The nucleus of both teams had played at Naples in 1951, when the Americans had won easily. But the Italians had obviously improved and they now had Belladonna and Avarelli in place of the Marmic pair. Jimmy Ortiz-Patino and I made our head-quarters just across the border in Switzerland.

For the first time South America, represented by Argentina, had a place in the Bermuda Bowl. The Argentine players had some winning sessions against both the other teams but were never quite in the running. For purposes of presentation, two matches were featured in each session. While we had used display boards, with Jumbo cards, for exhibition matches in Britain, this was the first time I had seen genuine bridgerama, with an electrically-operated board. It was a great success.

If the Italians have a fault in bidding, it is that some of their players tend to persist with their own long suits when it would be wiser to leave the decision to partner. This example occurred in the middle of the match when the Americans were fighting back after Italy had taken an early lead.

South dealer
N-S vulnerable

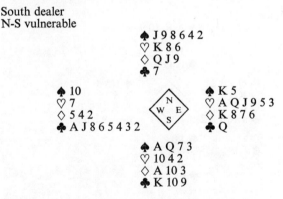

The bidding on bridgerama went as follows:

South	*West*	*North*	*East*
Roth	Chiaradia	Stone	D'Alelio
1 ♣	3 ♣	No (1)	3 ♡
No	4 ♣	4 ♠ (2)	Dble (3)
No	5 ♣ (4)	Dble	No
No	No		

(1) In accordance with the Roth-Stone theory that moderate hands ripen . . .

(2) . . . with age.

(3) A hard decision, to which D'Alelio found the best answer.

(4) Contrary to all general principles: he has already shown the character of his hand.

Chiaradia was three down, losing 500. His final call made a difference of 1,000, because the defence to 4 ♠ goes swimmingly— club lead, three rounds of hearts, overruff of a club by ♠ K.

As it happened, there was no swing on the board. At the other table, South opened 1 ♠. Becker overcalled with 4 ♣ and North bid 4 ♠. Silodor now bid 5 ♣; I think that many good players would have done the same.

On the tenth and last day, when the Americans were still within range, there was a slam that led to interesting play in both rooms.

West dealer
E-W vulnerable

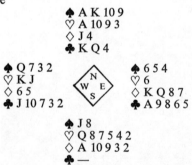

```
                    ♠ A K 10 9
                    ♡ A 10 9 3
                    ◇ J 4
                    ♣ K Q 4
    ♠ Q 7 3 2                      ♠ 6 5 4
    ♡ K J              N           ♡ 6
    ◇ 6 5          W     E         ◇ K Q 8 7
    ♣ J 10 7 3 2       S           ♣ A 9 8 6 5
                    ♠ J 8
                    ♡ Q 8 7 5 4 2
                    ◇ A 10 9 3 2
                    ♣ —
```

Crawford led a slightly deceptive ♣ 2 against 6 ♡ and D'Alelio went up with the queen from dummy. This was not good play, for one club discard could not help him, but two might. If he plays low from dummy, East, after the lead of ♣ 2, has a tough decision. Suppose that East plays the ace; South ruffs, leads a trump to the ace, returns to ◇ A and runs ♠ J, obtaining discards for four diamonds.

At the other table Rapee was also in 6 ♡ and Siniscalco led a diamond to the queen and ace. After a trump to the ace declarer led a low club from the table. This would have caught some players, but not Forquet, who judged that if South had held a club loser he would have played for a discard on the spades.

Italy finally won by 37 (old) I.M.P.s. I wrote at the time that the match had everything: drama, spectacle, excitement, intense, and not always cordial, rivalry.

It was interesting to learn, when in Italy, that the Italians had a grant from their government as well as from the municipality of Como. Imagine the British government contributing to such a cause! Of course, if it were a matter of organizing a display of folk dancing in a Yugoslavian village, the Arts Council would leap forward with public money.

Trials for the European that year were surprisingly brief. Schapiro and I were nominated as Probables for Oslo and a number of other players were formed into teams for trial matches. Some declined, because no promises were made that the winning team in the trials would be selected *en bloc*. After the first round, in which Gray and Truscott, R. and J. Sharples, won three matches of 32 boards, the selectors brought down the guillotine on the rest of the field, naming the team as early as March. Guy Ramsey, in the *Daily Telegraph*, expressed the hope that in the intervening period we would put a 'cutting edge' on our performance by playing a series of practice matches. We did in fact play three matches without sustaining the lack of team confidence that usually results from such exercises.

The story at Oslo was similar to Vienna. We had a good record, with nine wins, two draws and a narrow loss to Italy (a match we could easily have won). The final order was Italy, Britain, France.

For some reason, my mind is a bit blank about the Oslo tournament. Hands from the world championship in New York the following January are more familiar because of a lively account that the Swedish editor, Eric Jannersten, wrote for the *British Bridge World*. After reading that some of the Argentine players suffered from 'debut nervousity' and that in the match between Italy and

North America 'The both teams were strolling along side by side with U.S.A. half a stride ahead', who could ever again tolerate those threadbare phrases, 'beginners' nerves' or 'neck-and-neck'?

The Americans chose their team by a new method this year, pitting the winners of the Vanderbilt against the winners of the Spingold. (Odd that the Americans never seem to consider *selecting* their team; perhaps one day a group of helmeted warriors will volunteer for that task?) Fishbein's team won by 5 I.M.P.s over 112 boards, and the final line-up, after Lazard had been brought in from the losing team, was Fishbein-Hazen, Harmon-Stakgold, Lazard-Sam Fry Jr.

Play was level for the first three days. Then the Italians fell behind, mainly as a result of this unusual disaster:

West dealer
N-S vulnerable

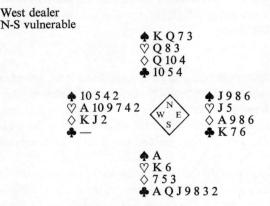

```
                    ♠ K Q 7 3
                    ♡ Q 8 3
                    ◇ Q 10 4
                    ♣ 10 5 4

♠ 10 5 4 2                      ♠ J 9 8 6
♡ A 10 9 7 4 2                  ♡ J 5
◇ K J 2                         ◇ A 9 8 6
♣ —                             ♣ K 7 6

                    ♠ A
                    ♡ K 6
                    ◇ 7 5 3
                    ♣ A Q J 9 8 3 2
```

This was the bidding in the closed room:

South	West	North	East
Belladonna	Harmon	Avarelli	Stakgold
1 ◇ (1)	1 ♡	1 ♠	1 NT
3 NT (2)	No	No	No

(1) 1 ♣ is conventional in the Roman system and 2 ♣ would have a different meaning altogether.

(2) A bid that few players would think of and still fewer would make.

West led a heart, which ran to the king. Declarer played off ace and another club, East won and returned a heart, on which South inadvertently dropped a diamond. Harmon was content with the 9, taken by the queen in dummy. At this point Avarelli queried the discard, Belladonna corrected the revoke, Harmon changed ♡ 9 to ♡ A, *but the queen had to remain on the table.* When West, after running his hearts, led a low diamond, Belladonna desperately went up with the queen and so finished six down.

The contract was made at the other table, but it is interesting to note that after South has played low from dummy on the first trick there is a possible defence. East wins the second or third club, then leads a heart; West takes the ace and exits immediately with a spade. Now South cannot run off his clubs without ruining the dummy.

The Italians are justly noted for their calm, but Belladonna was rattled by this catastrophe and the Americans at one point increased their lead to 29 (old) I.M.P.s. The next day was a different story, with Avarelli and Belladonna concerned in two more remarkable episodes. This was the first:

East dealer
Love all

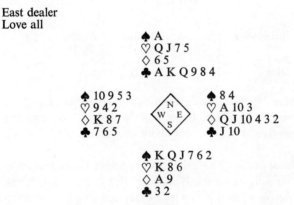

```
                        ♠ A
                        ♡ Q J 7 5
                        ◊ 6 5
                        ♣ A K Q 9 8 4
      ♠ 10 9 5 3                      ♠ 8 4
      ♡ 9 4 2              N           ♡ A 10 3
      ◊ K 8 7         W       E        ◊ Q J 10 4 3 2
      ♣ 7 6 5              S           ♣ J 10
                        ♠ K Q J 7 6 2
                        ♡ K 8 6
                        ◊ A 9
                        ♣ 3 2
```

When Hazen and Fishbein, on bridgerama, stopped in 4 ♠ there was a big groan, but closer examination showed that after a diamond lead there was no play for either 6 ♠ or 6 ♣. 6 ♡, conceivably, but you couldn't get there.

Or could you? At the other table Stakgold opened with a weak 2 ◊, Belladonna doubled, Avarelli bid 3 ◊, and after testing and rejecting both black suits they finished in 6 ♡, played by South.

The play was not exactly a lay-down. The declarer won the diamond lead and crossed to ♠ A. Unable to return to hand quickly, he played off three top clubs. East did his best by putting in ♡ 10. Belladonna overruffed, took a discard on ♠ K, and ran ♡ 6, earning what Jannersten called a 'strong applaud'.

Another hammer blow followed soon after:

West dealer
Love all

```
                    ♠ J 10 8 7 6 2
                    ♡ 8 4
                    ◇ 8 7
                    ♣ 10 9 2

      ♠ K Q 5              N           ♠ 9 3
      ♡ 10 3 2        W        E       ♡ Q 9 6 5
      ◇ A J 2              S           ◇ Q 9 5 4
      ♣ Q 8 5 4                        ♣ J 7 6

                    ♠ A 4
                    ♡ A K J 7
                    ◇ K 10 6 3
                    ♣ A K 3
```

South	West	North	East
Belladonna	Harmon	Avarelli	Stakgold
—	1 NT	No	2 ♣ (1)
No	2 ◇	No	No
Dble	No	No (2)	No

(1) Presumably 'Gladiator', requiring the opener to rebid 2 ◇.

(2) If you examine the implications of the bidding, it is impossible that partner should want to hear about your spades. Still, it was a fine pass.

The defence began with three rounds of hearts, North discarding a club, then a fourth heart, West discarding a spade and North ruffing. After ♠ A, ♣ A K and a club ruff, followed by a spade to the king, West was down to ◇ A J 2 and ♣ Q, while East and South had only trumps left. West cashed ◇ A, then ruffed a club with ◇ Q. South had to overruff and lead away from ◇ 10 6. The end-play saved a trick, but it was still 700. At the other table South opened 2 NT in fourth position and the American pair, apparently lacking the technical means to stop in 3 ♠, played in 4 ♠, down two.

The final session in the open room was televised, but the experiment was apparently not a success. Play was below standard on both sides, the Italians increasing their lead to win by 50 match points. Live television must seem very slow to the majority of viewers; it would surely be more sensible to record the session and show the highlights.

fifteen

TRAUMATIC END AT TURIN

In the early part of 1959 Norman Squire and I exchanged some correspondence in the *British Bridge World*, arising from my review of his book, *Guide to Bridge Conventions*. His remark, 'I cannot too strongly recommend that the natural path be followed', struck me as an amusing example of double-think. Not long before I had quoted this mystic utterance from one of his articles:

Technical explanation: jump-return preference is forcing to repeat-preference level. I can't go into that, but I hope to have a small work on Trump Support out one day.

I suggested that the robes he wore as the apostle of naturalism were spotted. The controversy got nowhere because in Squire's view any convention that belonged to his Theory of Bidding was immaculate.

I feel rather strongly about the general subject of book reviewing. Many bridge correspondents just pick up a phrase from the introduction or produce one of the standard soporifics such as 'A useful addition to your bridge library' or 'No player can fail to benefit . . .'. Apart from being discourteous to an author who has laboured for months, what service is this to readers? Then there is the Eternal Flattery syndrome. Ewart Kempson, in *Bridge Magazine*, and Harry Ingram, in the *Contract Bridge Journal*, lavished compliments on every book they mentioned. Another wretched practice, more common in America than in Britain, is the pre-publication potted praise. Author who has a book coming out phones colleague and says, 'My publishers would very much like an opinion from you about my new book.' Colleague, who knows what is expected and may want a favour himself one day, says 'I'm a bit busy just now, but I'm sure I'll go along with anything you'd like to say on my behalf.' So, when the book comes out, the back cover lists enthusiastic comments from half a dozen experts who have not even seen it.

Bert Dormer told me that when he worked for a year or two in America he found that authors expected a favourable review as a right. 'If you didn't praise them to the skies they acted as though you were trying to take the bread from their wife and kiddies.' The

Bridge World and the *A.C.B.L. Bulletin* are more critical nowadays; if you know how to assess their comments you can tell when they think a book is worthless. Many poor books are published, often at the author's own expense, and I don't see why the public should not be warned. Once I wrote in the *Observer*:

Contract Bridge in Twenty Lessons, by —— ——. This author should hasten to take them.

After the 1959 Gold Cup final the selectors nominated Schapiro and myself, and the Manchester pair, Franks and Lazarus, for the European Championship at Palermo, Sicily. The team was later completed by Meredith and Konstam. Reg Corwen was appointed captain but later had to withdraw for business reasons. He called me aside to reassure me on this point. 'I didn't want you to think I resigned because I thought you had no chance', he said; one of those things that might have been better put. Joel Tarlo took his place.

Franks and Lazarus were our best pair at Palermo. Schapiro suffered from a prevalent infection, and what with one thing and another the team performed less well than at Vienna or Oslo, finishing a moderate third to Italy and France. Despite this, I have the pleasantest memories of this championship. Hotel, food and climate were delightful; it was as pleasant to bathe at 2 a.m. as at midday. Indeed, you might say we were in luck to the finish. When we found our table at the banquet Joel observed: 'From here we shan't be able to hear the speeches.'

In one of Italy's matches there was an example of a line of thought in bidding that is generally overlooked. Chiaradia and Forquet held these cards:

West	East
♠ A K J 6 3	♠ Q 7 2
♡ A 4	♡ 10 2
◇ A K 7	◇ Q 8 5 3 2
♣ K Q J	♣ A 6 3

Playing the Neapolitan system, forerunner of the Blue Club, they bid as follows:

West	East
Forquet	Chiaradia
1 ♣ (1)	1 ♠ (2)
2 ♠	3 ♦
3 ♠	4 ♣
4 NT (3)	5 ♣ (4)
7 ♠ (5)	

(1) Conventional, usually 17 points or more.

(2) Showing two Neapolitan controls—either an ace or two kings.

(3) A general slam try, not Blackwood.

(4) Showing the control and accepting the slam invitation. If he had not held ♠ Q he would have signed off in 5 ♠.

(5) This is the interesting call. Forquet knows that his partner holds ♣ A, a diamond suit, ♠ Q, but no second round control in hearts. If the diamonds are jack high, and the suit does not run, a heart lead will beat six. When it is a question of making five or seven, it is right to bid seven.

The organization at Palermo lacked the smooth effectiveness of preceding tournaments. It was usually not until the middle of the following morning that Signor Rosa made the leisurely ascent of his ladder to enter results on the main scoreboard. Guy Ramsey remarked to me that the Italian telephone system was going to shorten his days. Alas, this was prophetic, for he had another heart attack and died the following month. Guy always took in very good part any little digs of mine at his literary or oratorical flights. On the Sunday after he died he was due to be heard in a recorded radio programme, the final of a bidding competition which he and his partner had won. In accordance with BBC policy, the programme was cancelled; a pity, for if they have radios in heaven nothing would have given him greater pleasure.

The first Olympiad was scheduled for Turin in 1960. Boris and I teamed up with Gardener and Rose, who in the past had usually been on the opposite side in trials. We won conclusively and the team was completed by Flint and Swimer, with Louis Tarlo as captain.

It is surprising to read that 'every West player' led ◇ 10 against 3 NT on the following hand from the team trial:

East dealer
Love all

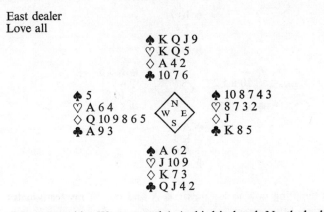

♠ K Q J 9
♡ K Q 5
◊ A 4 2
♣ 10 7 6

♠ 5
♡ A 6 4
◊ Q 10 9 8 6 5
♣ A 9 3

♠ 10 8 7 4 3
♡ 8 7 3 2
◊ J
♣ K 8 5

♠ A 6 2
♡ J 10 9
◊ K 7 3
♣ Q J 4 2

At most tables West opened 1 ◊ third in hand, North doubled, South responded 2 NT and North raised to 3 NT. If West leads ◊ 10 his partner's jack is allowed to hold the first trick and West cannot bring in the suit. To lead the queen would now be considered routine; it gains when either North or East holds a singleton jack.

There was an instructive point in this deal also:

South dealer
N-S vulnerable

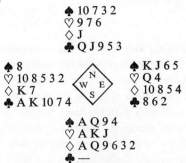

♠ 10 7 3 2
♡ 9 7 6
◊ J
♣ Q J 9 5 3

♠ 8
♡ 10 8 5 3 2
◊ K 7
♣ A K 10 7 4

♠ K J 6 5
♡ Q 4
◊ 10 8 5 4
♣ 8 6 2

♠ A Q 9 4
♡ A K J
◊ A Q 9 6 3 2
♣ —

South plays in 4 ♠ and West leads ♣ K (or ♣ A). The natural play is to ruff the club and lead a low diamond, won by West's king. West exits with a heart. South wins, ruffs a diamond and finesses ♠ Q, arriving at this position:

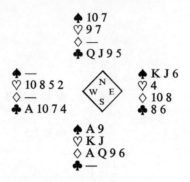

```
                    ♠ 10 7
                    ♡ 9 7
                    ◇ —
                    ♣ Q J 9 5
        ♠ —                        ♠ K J 6
        ♡ 10 8 5 2                 ♡ 4
        ◇ —                        ◇ 10 8
        ♣ A 10 7 4                 ♣ 8 6
                    ♠ A 9
                    ♡ K J
                    ◇ A Q 9 6
                    ♣ —
```

It is tempting now to lay down ♠ A and one of my team-mates committed that error. East, in time, ruffed the fifth diamond, drew the remaining trumps and led a club to his partner's ace.

In such positions, where the declarer can afford to lose two trump tricks and there is a danger that one opponent may hold the long trump, it is wrong to play off the master trump. Here South should continue to play on diamonds. If trumps are 3–2 nothing can happen to him. If they are 4–1 he still wins unless East began with a doubleton diamond. As the cards lie, East would ruff the fifth round but would make only one further trick.

The 30 teams at Turin were divided into three sections of ten, with two from each section qualifying for the final stage. We won every match in the qualifying round and met Italy in the first round of the final. We won a hard, close match by 8 points, having the better of the luck. Our next two matches were against American teams (America had three teams at Turin, because of the number of tournament players in the country) and we won both by good margins. An interesting point of play arose when a suit was distributed in this fashion:

```
              J 7 5
        A Q 3          10 8 4
              K 9 6 2
```

Looking for tricks at notrumps, the American declarer led low to the jack, which held. When he led back the 5 my partner went in with the 10, a clever false card. This was headed by the king and ace and the declarer, suspecting that Q 8 was over him, did not touch the suit again, though it would have provided him with a much-wanted ninth trick. When the deal was reported in the *British Bridge World* a correspondent pointed out that it was a mistake by South to cover the 10 with the king. East would not have let the jack win if he had held A 10 x, so the king could not gain; as the cards lay, West would have had to overtake. There are other situations where the same type of reasoning can be applied.

In the fourth round we lost our first match, to France, making mistakes in dummy play. When the last day began we were level with France on victory points and had a better quotient. At the end of the morning session (yes!) France was 9 up on Italy and we were 25 ahead against Goren (whose team was mostly Schenken and Ogust, Mathe and Allinger). These were old I.M.P.s, remember, so our lead by the present scale would have been from 35 to 40. At this stage you could scarcely have named the odds in our favour. We put on another 15 points at the beginning of the next session, but from then on everything went wrong. Our opponents played a fine, bustling game, and there were signs of weariness and over-anxiety in our camp. I still think, however, that we were unfortunate on the most discussed hand of the match:

South dealer
N-S vulnerable

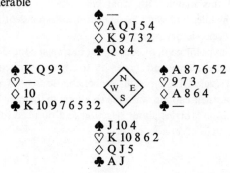

This was the bidding at my table:

South	West	North	East
Schenken	Schapiro	Ogust	Reese
1 ♡	2 ♣	2 NT (!)	No
3 NT	4 ♣	4 ♡	Dble
No	No	No	

Our opponents made two overtricks, while obviously we could have made thirteen tricks in spades by bringing down the doubleton ♣ A. Apparently, North's 2 NT was forcing in the system. If I had known that, I might have been more suspicious on the East hand. It did look as though I had good defence, the way the bidding had gone. Some critics said that West should have refused to defend on his unbalanced hand, but I don't agree with that; for him to take out into 4 ♠ would have been a wild shot.

The result was the more galling because at the other table Britain appeared to have a good board. Playing in 5 ♠, East ruffed the heart lead and led a low club from the table. North looked at this for a moment, wondering whether he should go in with the queen. Deciding against it, he played low. When the jack fell from South the declarer formed the notion that North held ♣ A x x and South Q J alone. When next in dummy he led ♣ K and could not thereafter make the contract.

We ended this match with what was called a winning draw. France, meanwhile, had gone far ahead of a despondent Italy and so beat us by one victory point.

It was a disappointment, of course, but one must concede that the French lasted best. They had three very strong and very equal pairs —Jais and Trézel, Ghestem and Bacherich, Bourchtoff and Delmouly, so that their captain was able to alternate them on a regular schedule, with no worries about selection and no need for anyone to play more than 40 boards a day.

sixteen

WIND OF CHANGE

From March to December 1961 every issue of the *British Bridge World* contained letters about the degree to which the probabilities of suit distribution change as the play develops. This is no academic matter: it is highly relevant to the play of many hands. Here is an example which presents the problem in basic form:

West	*East*
♠ A K 7 6 4 2	♠ J 5 3
♡ K 4	♡ A 10 6 5 2
◇ A Q 6	◇ 7 4
♣ A 7	♣ 9 6 4

Playing in 6 ♠, West wins the club lead, draws the trumps in two rounds and plays ♡ K and ♡ A, everybody following. He has to choose now between taking a diamond finesse or ruffing a third round of hearts; in effect, he must play for the hearts to be 3–3 or for South to hold ◇ K. Most players would take the diamond finesse. 'A 3–3 break in hearts is only a 36 per cent chance', they would say, 'and the diamond finesse is a 50 per cent chance.'

But that is wrong! Let us consider the heart suit on its own.

A 10 6 5 2
K 4

Most players know that, initially, a 4–2 break is more likely than 3–3. The probabilities, in round numbers, are 48 per cent for 4–2, 36 per cent 3–3, 15 per cent 5–1, 1 per cent 6–0.

But these odds are not static. Once both opponents have followed to the king and ace, the 5–1 and 6–0 distributions are eliminated. If we apply the same proportions, 48 to 36, to the chances that remain, we will find that the 4–2 break has become about a 57 per cent chance, 3–3 a 43 per cent chance.

There are, however, other ways of looking at it. With only two cards remaining, it can be argued that a 1–1 break is slightly more probable than 2–0. If that argument is right, then a 3–3 break has become at least a 52 per cent chance.

In a way, both these theories are correct. (If I seem to speak with certitude, it is not because I am a pundit in these matters but because I know who the pundits are. Colonel Roy Telfer of Plymouth and Alec Traub of South Africa are two who wrote with great authority on the subject.)

The nut of the matter is this: If opponents are supposed to be capable of all manner of false-carding, and if the play occurs early on, then the likelihood of a 3–3 break is at least 43 per cent; but if certain inferences can be drawn from the play of the opponents, the odds will often increase to at least 52 per cent. Also, the further the play has developed, the more likely (subject to special inferences from the bidding or play) are the even distributions. To take an extreme case, if there are six cards of a suit outstanding and at trick 10 none of these have appeared, they must necessarily be divided 3–3.

It may seem puzzling at first that the style of play by the opponents should have any bearing on the probabilities of distribution. The point becomes clear if we consider the common situation where opponents would not readily play a particular card, such as the queen when declarer's holding is:

A J 7 5 3
K 4

Planning to establish the suit by ruffing, South plays off the king and ace. All follow, but the queen, a *significant* card, has not appeared. In considering the possibilities that remain, declarer must reflect that not only are 5–1 and 6–0 distributions eliminated, but also those where the queen was doubleton. The suit was originally Q x x x opposite x x or Q x x opposite x x x. The second of these, Q x x opposite x x x, is more likely.

In practice, of course, defenders rarely discard at random. Many cards which are not strictly significant may appear so to a player who cannot see the complete hand. Players do not lightly drop queens and jacks on the first round of a suit. When these semi-significant cards do not appear, the likelihood of even distributions is increased. This is simply the converse of the obvious proposition that when an unexpectedly high card appears early on, you suspect that the player may have no more.

Let us look now at some other suit combinations where the odds can change in a surprising way.

(1) A K 8 6 5 4   (2) A Q J 6 5 4
       3   3

Here we have an interesting comparison. The chances of a 3–3 break is initially 36 per cent. In example (1) South plays off ace and king and all follow. Very little can be inferred from the cards played by good opponents; thus the probability of a 3–3 break is 43 per cent at least, but not much more. In (2) South finesses the queen successfully and cashes the ace. Here the king is a truly significant card. If it has not appeared, the probability that it will drop on the next round is not less than 52 per cent.

Now consider this familiar holding:

(3) A 10 7 5 3 2
     K J 9

Initially the chances for 3–1, 2–2 and 4–0 are 50 per cent, 40 per cent and 10 per cent. Both opponents follow to the king. Since a singleton queen has not appeared, we have to compare now the original probability of Q x opposite x x with Q x x opposite x. The 2–2 break is more likely and the expectation is in fact 52 per cent.

We have here a confirmation from experience of the theory we have been discussing. Most players know that 3–1 is a more likely division than 2–2, but they also know that, other things being equal, it is right to play for the drop of the queen with nine cards. The odds on a 2–2 break have altered when both opponents have followed to the first round and the significant queen has not appeared.

Compare these two situations where there is a seven-card remainder:

(4) A K 7 5 2   (5) A K J 5 2
       4   4

Initially, the chance of developing a long card by finding the suit 4–3 is 62 per cent. When all follow to the ace and king the chance of 4–3 as against 5–2 rises to (at least) 67 per cent in (1), to 74 per cent in (2) when the significant queen has not appeared in two rounds.

Obviously there is no need to memorize these percentages, but the general lesson is surely of practical importance—that the prospect of a level break increases as opponents follow to the early rounds, and increases more sharply when a significant card (one which an opponent would not play unless he had to) has not appeared.

The European Championship in 1961 was played at Torquay. I thought it would suit me better professionally to do the bridgerama commentary with Harold Franklin than to seek a place in the team. This was a wise decision, because the bridgerama in the beautiful setting of Torre Abbey was the success of the tournament; the playing rooms were cramped and unattractive.

As at Brighton in 1950, Britain carried off both the open and ladies' championships. Without in any way detracting from the fine performance of the open team (Priday-Truscott, Rose-Gardener, Konstam-Rodrigue), it must be said that many countries were drawing breath, as it were, after the exertions of Turin. Neither Italy nor France was represented by its top players. The Italians, nevertheless, were very impressive on occasions. I wrote an article for the *Bridge World* entitled 'Five-Board Slaughter', which described how they amassed a lead of 45–0 against Switzerland in the first five boards. This was Board 1:

South dealer
Love all

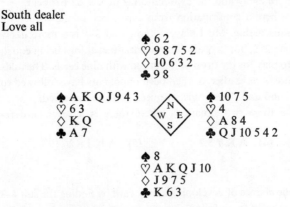

```
                    ♠ 6 2
                    ♡ 9 8 7 5 2
                    ◇ 10 6 3 2
                    ♣ 9 8

   ♠ A K Q J 9 4 3              ♠ 10 7 5
   ♡ 6 3              N         ♡ 4
   ◇ K Q          W     E       ◇ A 8 4
   ♣ A 7              S         ♣ Q J 10 5 4 2

                    ♠ 8
                    ♡ A K Q J 10
                    ◇ J 9 7 5
                    ♣ K 6 3
```

When bridgerama is used in an important event the players in the closed room start half an hour before those on bridgerama, so that spectators can see what has happened at the other table. With Italy North-South, the bidding was shown as follows:

South Cremoncini	West Bardola	North Mascheroni	East Jacobi
1 ♡	Dble	No	3 ♣
No	4 ♠	No	No
No			

It looks as though East might have made a move towards the slam, but he had already shown fair values. The sign-off in response to the double would have been 1 ♠ (Herbert convention) and 2 ♣ would have been 'positive'. So possibly West should have done more. However, the slam is not easy to reach after an adverse opening and it was unlikely, I commented, that there would be any swing. The bidding on bridgerama then unrolled as follows:

South Ortiz	West Brogi	North Bernasconi	East Bianchi
1 ♡	3 NT (1)	No	4 ◇ (2)
No	4 ♡ (3)	No	5 ♣ (4)
No	6 ♠	No	No
No			

(1) Showing the equivalent of an opening force and asking for aces.

(2) One ace.

(3) Asking about control in hearts.

(4) Second-round control in hearts.

Nice to have the machinery when such a hand comes along!

Board 4 was another cruel blow for Switzerland.

East dealer
Game all

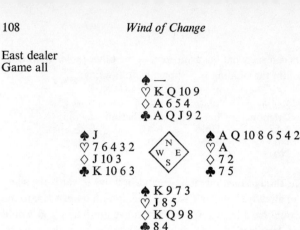

```
                        ♠ —
                        ♡ K Q 10 9
                        ◇ A 6 5 4
                        ♣ A Q J 9 2
    ♠ J                                ♠ A Q 10 8 6 5 4 2
    ♡ 7 6 4 3 2         N              ♡ A
    ◇ J 10 3         W     E           ◇ 7 2
    ♣ K 10 6 3          S              ♣ 7 5
                        ♠ K 9 7 3
                        ♡ J 8 5
                        ◇ K Q 9 8
                        ♣ 8 4
```

In the closed room the Italians had the chance to double 4 ♠ and collect 800, but instead they bid 5 ◇ and made it. On bridgerama:

South	West	North	East
Ortiz	Brogi	Bernasconi	Bianchi
—	—	—	1 ♠
No	1 NT	Dble	2 ♠ (!)
Dble	No	No	No

South led ◇ K against 2 ♠ doubled. Best defence beats the contract by one trick, but the play must be well timed. South switches to a club at trick 2, North wins and returns a low diamond to the queen. South leads a second club. At this stage a further club from North promotes a second trump trick for the defence, but North may seek to establish a heart trick first. Probably the right card is ♣ A. Anyway, the Swiss muddled the defence, though not quite in this fashion. The swing of 1,270 cost 17 I.M.P.

The present scale of I.M.P. was used for the first time at Torquay. I had forgotten that Britain at first opposed the change, which indeed was no improvement on the old scale. It was also suggested at the time that victory points should be awarded on quotient rather than margin: to win by 50–25 is obviously more meritorious than to win by 100–75. This sensible idea has not been revived.

The match between Britain and Italy contained a celebrated hand:

West dealer
E-W vulnerable

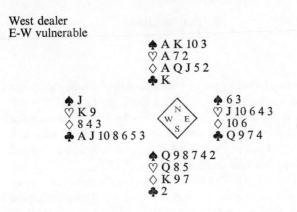

♠ A K 10 3
♥ A 7 2
♦ A Q J 5 2
♣ K

♠ J
♥ K 9
♦ 8 4 3
♣ A J 10 8 6 5 3

♠ 6 3
♥ J 10 6 4 3
♦ 10 6
♣ Q 9 7 4

♠ Q 9 8 7 4 2
♥ Q 8 5
♦ K 9 7
♣ 2

Gardener and Rose, on bridgerama, had an unimpressive sequence. After a pass by West, North opened 2 ♦, forcing for one round, and South chose to respond 3 ♦. North bid 3 ♠ and South 4 ♠, where they rested.

The excitement occurred in the closed room, where the bidding went:

South	West	North	East
Cremoncini	Priday	Mascheroni	Truscott
—	3 ♣	Dble	No
4 ♠	No	5 ♣	No
7 ♠	No	No	No

The explanation of the final call was linguistic: Cremoncini meant to contract for 6 ♠, but his limited English unseated him. Priday was unaware of this, of course, and not wanting ♣ A to be ruffed he led the 'safe' ♠ J. South now drew trumps, ran five diamonds, and followed with the rest of the spades, squeezing West in hearts and clubs. Despite this reverse, Britain won the match 6–0.

There was a daily *Bulletin* at Torquay for the first time since Stockholm, where the latitude allowed to correspondents had earned the disapproval of the authorities. I expect it was from the *Bulletin* that I culled this vignette:

As Others See Us

Two elderly ladies in a Torquay hotel lounge:
'That was Mr Priday; such a nice gentleman.'
'Oh, I agree with you, dear. I was so surprised to find he was one of the bridge players.'

LITTLE MAJOR

In the middle of 1962 I gave up the editorship of the *British Bridge World* and was succeeded by Albert Dormer. 'Editors', I wrote when signing off, 'like headmasters and chief constables, are a breed who should move on from time to time. Otherwise one falls into too much of a routine, there is a lack of freshness, and occasional faults become standard faults.'

The first World Pairs Olympiad was held in Cannes at about this time. Schapiro and I had an experience similar to Turin. We led the field from the 7th to the 9th session but were overtaken in the final furlong. Having scored under average on the last day we were quite relieved to finish second to Jais and Trézel, the only pair among the leaders to return a good score. Mrs Markus and Mrs Gordon won both the Ladies Pairs and the Mixed Teams, playing respectively with Gardener and Schapiro.

I had enjoyed being on the sidelines at Torquay and did not compete in the trials for Beirut. Somewhat to my surprise, since the B.B.L. selectors have a habit of appointing one another to the post, I was asked to captain the open team. A young pair, Peter Swinnerton-Dyer and Ken Barbour, had won the long pairs trial so easily that in another medium there would have been a Stewards Inquiry. Both, unfortunately, have been lost to the tournament game in Britain, Barbour working in America and Swinnerton-Dyer pursuing a distinguished academic career. Swinnie was noted for the eccentricity of his answers to the *British Bridge World* bidding competitions and for droll remarks at the table. Having entered 900, 1,100 and 2,800 in the opponents' column, he observed: 'I did not come to play in these Trials in my capacity as a senior wrangler.'*

In Beirut the team made a bad start, losing 6–0 to Switzerland. Italy beat us 4–2 in a high-class match, but we were still in the fight when we met the leaders, France, in the eighth round. I had taken the bold step of playing Swinnerton-Dyer and Barbour in the first half, and this was board 4:

---

* A high mathematical distinction.

North dealer
Game all

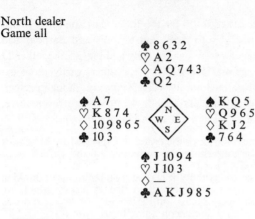

♠ 8 6 3 2
♡ A 2
♢ A Q 7 4 3
♣ Q 2

♠ A 7
♡ K 8 7 4
♢ 10 9 8 6 5
♣ 10 3

♠ K Q 5
♡ Q 9 6 5
♢ K J 2
♣ 7 6 4

♠ J 10 9 4
♡ J 10 3
♢ —
♣ A K J 9 8 5

With Barbour North, the bidding went:

South	West	North	East
—	—	1 ♢	No
2 ♣	No	2 ♢	No
2 ♠	No	4 ♠	No
No	No		

The raise to 4 ♠ would be considered unwise today, as South's 2 ♠ in this sequence might be a notrump probe on a 3-card suit.

West opened a heart and dummy won. South appears to have three trumps and a heart to lose, but Swinnie showed how such hands should be managed. He began with three rounds of clubs, West ruffing with the 7 and North overruffing. Then came a diamond ruff and a fourth club. West ruffed with the ace (best) and dummy's heart went away.

West exited with a diamond and South ruffed in hand. After a heart ruff ♢ A dropped the king and ♢ Q was ruffed high by East. A high spade was cashed, but declarer had to win the last two tricks, either making a spade and a club or his two trumps separately. The bidding and play followed a similar course at the other table, so there was no swing.

After leading at half time we lost this match and finished third equal with Switzerland, behind France and Italy. My captaincy did not go unscathed. Ewart Kempson, in *Bridge Magazine*, expressed the opinion that Konstam and Joel Tarlo had been asked to bear far too much of the brunt of battle and that Swinnerton-Dyer and

Barbour had been asked to do far too little. Harrison-Gray joined
in the attack. I was able to reply that Swinnie and Barbour had
played in every match except against Italy and played altogether 13
half sessions as against 15 and 16 by the other, vastly more experienced, pairs. I pointed out also that Kempson, though present,
had watched none of the play, while Gray was not even there.
Konstam contributed his support in the *British Bridge World*:

> I read with some annoyance the criticism expressed by Mr Ewart
> Kempson recently concerning the captaincy of the British open
> team in Beirut.
> I think it only fair to say that the team were unanimous in thinking
> Terence Reese equal to the best captain Britain has ever had. He
> watched practically every board—in itself a tedious task—and was
> at all times most helpful and encouraging to the team.

Towards the end of this year Boris and I played in the first of the
popular Canary Island tournaments. In the aeroplane going over,
the Little Major was born. Since I still get many inquiries about this
bidding system, it must contain some macabre interest.

It had seemed to me for some while that if one approached the
whole subject of bidding without preconceptions there was no reason
why, to indicate a spade suit, a player should bid 1 ♣, or, to indicate
a heart suit, 1 ♡. (That idea is contained, of course, in the widely
used transfer bids over 1 NT.) It must, in general, save a round of
bidding if you start with a lower call to indicate your real suit. In
the Little Major an opening bid of 1 ♣ signifies a heart suit, an
opening 1 ◊ either a spade suit or a strong no trump. Our first idea
for 1 ♡ and 1 ♠ was to use these bids in a purely obstructive sense
—on one, two or three cards in a limited hand. That is how the
system gained its name. We soon found, however, that it was impossible to dispense with these bids in a constructive role. The
system underwent many changes, but the general picture at the end
of two years was as follows:

1 ♣   In principle, a heart suit. To this, 1 ◊ is a negative
        response but may also be the first move on a big hand.
        (This duality, by the way, can easily be attached to any
        of the modern 1 ♣ systems.)

1 ◊   Either a spade suit or a 16–19 no trump. 1 ♡ is a nega-
        tive response but may also be the first move on a big
        hand.

1 ♡	Either a strong hand, usually 20 points upwards, or a controlled psychic on balanced hands in the 3 to 6 range.
1 ♠	Limited opening with length in both minors.
1 NT	Normal no trump type, 13 to 15 throughout.
2 ♣ 2 ◇	Limited opening, 12 to 15 with a fair minor suit, no 4-card major.
2 ♡ 2 ♠	Fairly strong major-minor two-suiter.
2 NT	Equal to a weak 3-bid in a minor or a strong minor 2-suiter.

This is just an outline of the opening sequences; there is a fuller (but by no means comprehensive) account in *Bridge for Tournament Players*. For slam bidding the Little Major was less well equipped than modern Precision with asking bids, but it was very strong in the game and part-score area and created many problems for the opponents.

When the Little Major first came into the news, there were many to remind me that I had long campaigned against artificial systems. Those critics missed the point. I wanted to show what the game would be like if no controls were exercised.

The English Bridge Union does not allow new systems to be played in domestic events, so opportunities to practise the Little Major were limited. However, Schapiro and I finished only 1 point behind Jais and Trézel in the first *Sunday Times* Pairs, and Flint and I won the team trials for Baden-Baden in 1963. At the end of this trial Flint, Schapiro and I were chosen from the winners, Harrison Gray, Konstam and J. Tarlo from the runners-up. This created the usual furore, mainly because Swinnerton-Dyer and Barbour, who had played in my team during the final round, had been passed over, despite many good performances. A month or two later they added fuel to the protests by winning the Gold Cup.

There was much rivalry in those days between the established internationals, known unflatteringly as the 'season-ticket holders', and the younger players, who of course had their successes from time to time. When someone wrote that our young players were some way behind those of France and America, Jimmy Tait, who contributed many amusing articles to the *British Bridge World*, declared that he could produce a dozen pairs from the younger set who could give the over-fifties a good match. In my poetic role I replied:

> I'd give up half my salary
> To play against the Tait Gallery.

As a matter of fact, a lot of nonsense is talked about experience. To perform well in the European Championship, it is not necessary, or a particular advantage, to have experience of the championship itself; all that is needed, apart from ability, is a few years' experience of good class play. On the other hand, it is equally nonsensical to talk of the importance of having young players with the stamina to sustain a fortnight's play. If you look round at the end of a long weekend of trials you will find that it is the younger players who wilt, while the older ones, used to playing every day, will be looking for a game of rubber bridge.

The field at Baden-Baden was below standard and the British team had one of its best years, winning every match. The Little Major created a great deal of interest among the Continental journalists—especially when in one match Boris and I abandoned it at half time, reverting to old-fashioned Acol.

The next big event was the 1964 Olympiad in New York. The B.B.L. announced that trials would be held to discover a team that would challenge the Baden-Baden winners. For some reason this trial never got off the ground and the same team went to New York. There the field was divided into two sections, with two teams qualifying from each section. We won our section and were drawn against Italy in the semi-final. We lost this match by 8 points and Italy went on to beat America in the final. An Australian writer, J. N. R. Griffiths, in a series called 'Hand from the Past', commented on the difficulty of judging what might happen at the 'other table', and continued as follows:

After the following hand was played by Britain against Italy in the 1964 Olympiad we can feel sure that no one anticipated the result when replayed in the other room.

North dealer
Love all

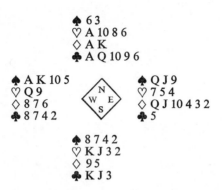

```
                    ♠ 6 3
                    ♡ A 10 8 6
                    ◇ A K
                    ♣ A Q 10 9 6
    ♠ A K 10 5                      ♠ Q J 9
    ♡ Q 9            ┌───────┐      ♡ 7 5 4
    ◇ 8 7 6         │N      │      ◇ Q J 10 4 3 2
    ♣ 8 7 4 2       │W    E │      ♣ 5
                    │   S   │
                    └───────┘
                    ♠ 8 7 4 2
                    ♡ K J 3 2
                    ◇ 9 5
                    ♣ K J 3
```

In both rooms South played 4 ♡. The Italian West led ♠ K, then played ♠ A and switched to a diamond. Declarer played ♡ A and ran the 10, making four. It is hard to see how an appreciable swing could occur.

In the other room Reese (West) led ♠ K, but Schapiro played ♠ Q, won the second round with ♠ J and led a third round, ruffed in dummy. When Forquet now played ♡ A and ran the 10 (not the best play) Reese won and led a fourth round of spades! Dummy ruffed with the 8, but Schapiro discarded his singleton club and declarer could not leave the table without allowing East a club ruff.

Truly a magnificent defence by the great English pair.

Well, thank you; but it all happened without premeditation; when there is no likelihood of tricks in the side suits the only sensible game is to attack the declarer's trump holding.

After one committee had said no, and another yes, the E.B.U. finally granted the Little Major an 'A' licence, which meant that it could be played in certain restricted events. This licence was withdrawn after two years, on the grounds that not enough players were playing the system to justify its renewal. We had to abandon it then, because it was not practicable to play a complicated system just in the few events to which the restrictions did not apply. It was, I know, unreasonable to expect that the Little Major would discourage the playing of artificial systems. We have seen in the larger world of science that clever inventions, however disagreeable their consequences, are seldom buried by an effort of will.

eighteen

PUG AND THE STRIPE-TAILED APE

The British victory at Baden-Baden gave Britain the right, as European champions, to play in what was technically the 1964 Bermuda Bowl contest, held at Buenos Aires early in 1965. The team that had played at Baden-Baden and New York was invited to represent the country again, but some of the players were not too happy about the way the partnerships had been lined up, the offer was declined, and trials were held. Flint and I, playing the Little Major, won by a good margin, Schapiro and Konstam were second, and after much manoeuvring the team was completed by Harrison-Gray and Albert Rose.

Most readers will know in outline what occurred in Buenos Aires. On the last day, after we had lost heavily to Italy but were favourites to be second, ahead of the USA and Argentina, Boris and I were accused of exchanging illegal signals by the way we held our cards. It was ironical that this should have happened after a week in which we had played far below our normal form. My account of the affair, together with the proceedings of the Foster-Bourne inquiry and all the hands that were adduced by both sides, is related in my book, *Story of an Accusation*, and I do not propose to add to it here or to seek to have any last words. At most, I will comment on some external developments.

Frederic Raphael, the novelist, whose father played at Crockford's and who reviewed my book for the *New Statesman*, remarked to me that I played it all very close to my chest. That was deliberate; to have described my own thoughts would have introduced a new dimension and destroyed the balance of the story I was trying to tell. I can say now, however, that in my perverse way I found the proceedings of the inquiry intensely interesting. It is worth remarking, too, that while no doubt some people were reserving their judgement, I encountered no instance of discourtesy, either at home or abroad.

One consequence of the affair—and I have not wavered from this view despite considerable pressure—was that it became impossible for Boris and myself to continue as a regular partnership. We were truly impaled on a fork. If we played together and did well it would be said that we had thought up something new, and if we did badly the same people would say, 'Look what happens when they have no cheating method.'

There were repercussions from Buenos Aires in the selection of British teams for the next three years. After a long pairs trial for Dublin in 1967 the six leading pairs were formed into two teams of six, team A consisting of Flint-Priday, Collings-Cansino, North-Pugh; team B of Gray-Stanley, Swimer-Goldstein, Hiron-Rose. Team A won decisively, but the selectors then nominated the first four from team A and Swimer-Goldstein from team B. This was not a clever move, for Flint and Swimer had given evidence for opposite sides during the Inquiry and it was known that relations were strained. Furthermore, in terms of statistics—for what those are worth—the performance of Swimer-Goldstein had been no better than that of North-Pugh and was well behind that of Gray-Stanley ($+$ 18 in the final trial as compared with $+$ 97). Immediately there were resignations and non-acceptors, and to complete the team the selectors had to go outside the six pairs who had qualified for the final stage. Newspapers seized on the affair with headlines such as 'Rebel group of bridge players', 'Row over national team', 'Bridge League threat of five-year ban'.

The Contract Bridge Association of Ireland invited me to do the bridgerama commentary at Dublin. In an article for the American *Bridge World* I described three hands from the championship under the title, 'A Little Learning'. This was one of them:

East dealer
N-S vulnerable

```
                    ♠ 9 8 5 3
                    ♡ K 5
                    ◇ 9 7 3 2
                    ♣ 10 9 4
  ♠ —                                ♠ Q J 10 4 2
  ♡ 8 6 3              N             ♡ Q 10 4 2
  ◇ Q J 10 8 5     W     E           ◇ 6 4
  ♣ A K 8 5 3         S             ♣ J 6
                    ♠ A K 7 6
                    ♡ A J 9 7
                    ◇ A K
                    ♣ Q 7 2
```

In the match between Israel and Ireland South at both tables
opened 2 NT. The Israeli West judged this to be the moment for the
unusual no trump and overcalled with 3 NT! As he had the lead
against notrumps and there was a chance that the opponents would
play in spades and run into a bad break, this was surely ill-advised.
His side eventually played in 4 ♣ doubled and did well to get out
for 300.

On bridgerama South played in 3 NT. The Irish West led a club
to the jack and queen. Declarer's first move was to lay down ♠ A,
on which West discarded a heart.

South has eight tricks on top if he assumes the heart finesse to be
right, and the best play at this point is to exit with a club. If West
cashes all his clubs East will be squeezed in the major suits. If West
takes only four rounds of clubs declarer will need to finesse ♡ 9 on
the second round and then end-play East to force a lead into ♡ A J.

The Israeli declarer surprised everyone by crossing to ♡ K at
once and finessing the 9 on the way back. Of course, it wasn't good
technique to cut himself off from dummy in this way. However, he
now cashed ◊ A and belatedly exited with a club. This was the
position after the fourth round of clubs:

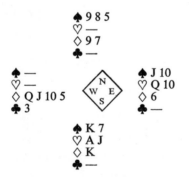

West knew declarer held ◊ K, so his partner would have a safe
discard on the fifth club and South himself would be embarrassed.
But West knew all about suicide squeezes and led a diamond. Then
South, recovering from his previous error, executed the end-play
against East.

Italy won by a distance this year, France was second and Britain
third. As usual, the championship had its extra-curricular comedies.

An elderly lady approached me one day and said in a strong Irish accent:

'Where would you be finding the better players—in the open room or the closed room?'

'The beginners are kept in the closed room,' I told her gravely, waving a hand in the direction of Bobby Slavenburg, current world pairs champion, who was about to enter the sanctum.

East is East and West is West. A Czech player was heard to say:

'We are very happy with our hotel. It is comfortable and only forty-five minutes' walk away.'

Britain did not send a team to the Olympiad at Deauville in 1968 because, while the European Bridge League had voted unanimously to accept the Foster-Bourne report, the World Bridge Federation had not done so. At Deauville the W.B.F. declared that the matter was closed.

In 1969 the European Championship was held at Oslo. Players entered in pairs and after a preliminary stage were formed into teams by the selectors. Flint and I played with L. Tarlo and Rodrigue. This was a good hand both for attack and defence:

North dealer
Love all

```
                  ♠ A K Q 9 5 2
                  ♡ 10 4
                  ◇ A 10 8
                  ♣ 7 3
  ♠ 8 6 4                        ♠ J 7 3
  ♡ A 9 7 3          N          ♡ 8 6 2
  ◇ Q 7 2        W     E        ◇ K 6 4 3
  ♣ K 9 6           S           ♣ A 10 5
                  ♠ 10
                  ♡ K Q J 5
                  ◇ J 9 5
                  ♣ Q J 8 4 2
```

Flint and I played in 2 ♠, making three, but the opponents at the other table reached 3 NT. Declarer won the first trick with the ♡ 10. What next?

In practice a heart was returned to the queen and ace. Rodrigue and Tarlo then played a smart defence: they cashed ♣ A and ♣ K, then exited with a spade. If dummy wins (at the table South let it run to his 10 without success) there will be two diamonds to lose at the finish.

The best play for South—not all that obvious—is to cash three spades before leading the second heart. Unable now to exit in spades, the defence cannot avoid establishing a ninth trick for the declarer.

A bidding problem from the same session:

South dealer
N-S vulnerable

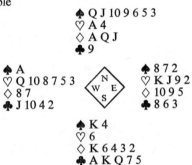

```
                    ♠ Q J 10 9 6 5 3
                    ♡ A 4
                    ◇ A Q J
                    ♣ 9
    ♠ A                           ♠ 8 7 2
    ♡ Q 10 8 7 5 3                ♡ K J 9 2
    ◇ 8 7                         ◇ 10 9 5
    ♣ J 10 4 2                    ♣ 8 6 3
                    ♠ K 4
                    ♡ 6
                    ◇ K 6 4 3 2
                    ♣ A K Q 7 5
```

The bidding begins:

South	West	North	East
1 ◇	3 ♡	5 ♠	?

What would you say now on the East hand? John Pugh, playing with Freddie North, made a bright bid, I thought: he doubled 5 ♠! The declarer made an overtrick, scoring 1,050, but this was a good save as compared with 1,430 for 6 ♠ or 1,300 for a sacrifice in 7 ♡. The double was of the variety known as 'stripe-tailed ape', so called because the doubler intends to flee like a stripe-tailed ape if there is a redouble.

The expected gain did not arise because at the corresponding table Priday and Gardener had the misfortune to arrive at 7 ♠ on the North-South cards and the further misfortune to do so while Boris Schapiro was watching. As the board went out of play, Boris made a tour of the four playing rooms to make the following little speech:

'Priday and Gardener were unlucky on one hand. They bid a grand slam and the ace of trumps was on the wrong side. Bad luck. Could happen to anyone.'

Our team finished the first of three weekends 10 victory points ahead of the field, but Flint and I were not fated to continue. In the month or so before the second round the celebrated case of Swimer *v* Mrs Markus came to court. This was a libel action, arising from a sentence in an article under Rixi's name that had appeared in the American *Bridge World* a few months after Buenos Aires. The sentence was to the effect that she, Mrs Markus, would not care to play under a captain who would join others in an accusation against members of his own team. The sentence contained an unfortunate word, conspiracy, and Swimer considered that he had been libelled.

The most famous libel lawyers in the country were engaged on the two sides. Rixi's main defence was that she had not intended publication of the sentence to which exception was taken: she had been in correspondence with Sonny Moyse, then editor of the *Bridge World*, and while she had given him general authority to publish her opinions she had certainly not authorized him to print the sentence to which exception was taken.

Rixi was not the most responsive of witnesses. She was there to have her say, and she had it, despite the admonitions of her own counsel, the protests of the other side, and the instructions of the judge. She had several letters which she had exchanged with Moyse and she read them all. It seemed to me that this correspondence showed her in a very good light: it was evident that she was sincere and did not attribute base motives to the people who had brought the charges at Buenos Aires. The jury contained three women and I formed the opinion that they would surely be on Rixi's side.

The judge's summing-up seemed to Rixi's friends to be most unfavourable. Perhaps one always thinks that when one's emotions are engaged, I don't know. He left the jury with a number of questions to answer, the first being whether the Defendant had authorized publication of the words which, he ruled, were libellous.

The jury retired and a long, long wait followed. After several hours there were signs of activity, but when we went into court we found that the jury had been recalled at the judge's request. The foreman reported that they were still debating the first of the questions they had to answer. An hour later they returned again, to report that they had made no progress. The judge explained how inconvenient it would be for everyone if they were unable to agree: was there any assistance he could give them? The foreman looked doubtful and a woman in the second row spoke up unexpectedly:

'It's no use, my Lord. We're never going to agree.'

'Be silent, madam,' said the judge sharply. 'Only the foreman is allowed to speak for you.'

'I'm afraid it's true,' said the foreman.

And there it ended. The plaintiff had the right to bring the case again, but he did not do so and became responsible for the costs of both sides.

What had all this to do with the trials, you ask. Well, although all parties had stressed that the truth or otherwise of the allegations made at Buenos Aires were not an issue in the case, Swimer during his evidence several times repeated his conviction that the charges were well founded. Inevitably, this led to much unwelcome publicity.

The B.B.L., obviously, could not control the way in which Swimer presented his case, but it was felt that they ought to have made some pronouncement about his participation in the trials. What would the atmosphere be like when we had to play against one another, and what would happen if our teams finished first and second, which was not unlikely? With my partner's agreement, I decided to withdraw, and without any prompting from me three other players did the same. Substitutes were brought in, the trials continued with five teams instead of six, and the team that finally went to Oslo finished ninth.

The main excitement at Oslo occurred in the final round of the women's championship. Britain began this round one victory point ahead of France. Britain was reported to have lost 3–5 to Denmark, while France lost 2–6 to Greece; thus Britain went up on the board as champions. However, the players in the open room had exceeded the time limit by 13 minutes, and in the last round of the tournament (when obviously there would be no point in a warning) this carried the heavy penalty of two victory points. It was admitted that the tournament director, a Norwegian, had twice spoken to the players, but neither they nor the team captain fully appreciated the danger. It was not until the next day that the omission to deduct penalty points was brought to the notice of the Appeals Committee. Two victory points were subtracted and the French were declared winners, as their quotient of match-points was better than Britain's.

'In an attempt to remove some of the bitterness from the prize-giving', wrote Harold Franklin in the *Bridge Magazine*, 'the French team accepted a suggestion to renounce the title, and though they received the first prizes no Ladies' Champion was announced for 1969.'

The telex machine had a moment of empathy when reporting one of Ireland's matches: 'At half-time the Irish led by one pint.'

nineteen

THEY DON'T GROW ON TREES

I suppose it is a sign of advancing years that comparatively recent events should seem less vivid than many that happened a long time ago. I look at the magazines of 1969 and 1970 and see reports of trials, championships, Gold Cup, Crockford's Cup, Masters Pairs, Spring Foursomes, Juan-Les-Pins, Deauville, and many others. Did I really play in all those, even win a few of them? I remember very little about it.

I have a good reason, at least, to remember the *Guardian* Tournament at the Europa Hotel in the spring of 1969. During the pairs I observed Maurice Weissberger (known as 'the Vice', because of his name and because he has been vice-captain of women's teams) playing with a very pretty girl. Pretty girls don't grow on trees at bridge tournaments and I thought it my duty to inquire into the matter. I was saved the trouble because at the next interval Maurice brought her over and introduced her: Alwyn Sherrington. I discovered that she lived in Blackpool and that we had common friends there. I mentioned that I would be up that way for the Open at Lytham in July, staying with the Robinsons, very well known in Lancashire bridge. She said she would call me at their home. She did, too, and we astonished the natives by playing in the local duplicate.

Later in the year Alwyn moved to London and we arranged to be married the following January. At this time Alwyn was engaged in opening a new branch of her firm in Manchester. On the day before the impending nuptials the head of the firm, an admirer, spent hours trying to dissuade her from the venture. Finally she weakened and rang me at the Eccentric Club in London, where I was playing rubber bridge. Perhaps it was all a mistake, was I absolutely sure, etc. According to her story, I replied, 'Not now, dearest, I am in the middle of a hand.' Whereupon she replaced the receiver and said, 'That settles it. I am going to marry that man.'

Most of the bridge wives smother their husbands in admiration, taking their part in every little argument that may arise at the bridge table or away from it. Alwyn is not like that. If I went to play in a world championship she wouldn't ask me on my return whether I had won or lost; she would have some interesting piece of news about the housework, though. It suits me that way; I have been lucky beyond all expectation or desert.

Better than any of my own adventures at this time, I recall the match of 80 rubbers played at the Piccadilly Hotel between the Omar Sharif Bridge Circus (Omar Sharif, Claude Delmouly, Leon Yallouze, Giorgio Belladonna, Benito Garozzo) and the British partnership of Jeremy Flint and Jonathan Cansino. The match was played for very high stakes—£1 a point with an additional £1,000 on every four rubbers. Most of the play was presented on bridgerama and the idea was that episodes should be filmed and offered as a television series in America.

As an entertainment for the home audience it was a great success, but I must say I thought from the first that the idea of a fortune from television rights was pie in the sky. It would probably be a year before the estimated 12 episodes could be trimmed into shape and offered to the public, and by that time who would be interested in a rubber bridge match played between British and Continental players, most of them not well known to the American public at large?

As things turned out, this issue was not put to the test. Just one pilot programme was prepared, and Omar was not pleased with that. The *Sunday Times*, some months after the match, printed a very frank article indeed about the young men who promoted the venture. In retrospect, it seems extraordinary that such an expensive project should have been launched without any guarantees. Clever bridge players are not necessarily clever businessmen.

As a match, it was an excellent contest. The Circus was ahead for most of the time and finally won by 5,470. Considering all the circumstances, the standard of play was extremely high. One hand, played by Omar, was of the quiz type:

West	*East*
♠ A J 8 3 2	♠ —
♡ A 9 3	♡ K Q 8
◇ K 9 6	◇ 7 5 4 3
♣ 7 3	♣ A Q J 10 6 4

West is in 3 NT and North leads ♠ K. How should West plan the play?

First, he should not hold up in spades, because the defenders may switch to a diamond and make three diamonds, a spade and a club. Then, having won with ♠ A, West should play a club to the ace: he does not mind losing a club trick to North and can guard against a singleton king in the South hand. Omar made the first safety play but disdained the second.

The match proved that a rubber bridge contest of this kind can be a great attraction. The play was faster than in tournament play and the fact that most spectators had an interest, emotional or financial, added a new dimension to bridgerama.

After the fracas that had upset the trials in 1969, and before that in 1967, the B.B.L. opened the 1969–70 season with a general declaration that the selectors aimed to create a team capable of working harmoniously as a team. The Council went on to lay down three conditions for all trialists: (1) that the B.B.L. was the sole judge whether individuals or pairs were fit and proper persons to represent the country and that anyone who agreed to become a candidate must undertake to play in a team with any other candidate; (2) that failure to participate fully in the trials would render a player liable to disciplinary action; and (3) that players must undertake not to communicate with the press on any contentious matter without written consent. Reasonable enough, but if the selectors would do their job in choosing a friendly team, none of the rest would arise.

As it turned out, the trials for Estoril in 1970 passed off without incident. My team (Flint-Reese, Cansino-Milford) finished level with Pugh in the final stage and the selectors chose our four plus Gordon-Pugh. Slam bidding throughout the team was poor during the championship and we finished fifth. Flint and I were playing the Blue Club at this time. We understood it well enough in theory— I had written a book on it and he had played with some of the Italians —but from time to time we came across situations where neither of us was quite sure what a particular bid would mean or what was the best action to take.

This prompted the reflection that it needs long, long practice to play a new method at championship level. Old-fashioned Acol has some unsatisfactory areas, particularly when the opener begins with 2 ♣ or an Acol two bid, but when one has played a system for 20 years or more all situations are familiar. There may be no perfect answer at a given point, but one knows from experience what is best within the system. People often ask how it is that the Italians have had such a long run at the top of world bridge. They have a few out-standing players, to be sure, but often only one or two of these has turned out for the European, and Italy has still won. The main reason, I am certain, is that they can play their systems day after day at rubber bridge. In the London clubs a pair is not allowed to play any specialized system, the principle being that the weaker players must not be put at any disadvantage.

In 1972 most of the top players turned to the Precision system, partly for professional reasons. The asking bids that follow a positive response to 1 ♣ are certainly an advance, but the system has a weakness in my opinion: the range of the negative response, 0–7, is too wide, and problems arise in competitive bidding at a low level. I prefer to use the 1 ♡ response of the Blue Club, signifying 6 points or more with less than three Neapolitan controls (2 for an ace, 1 for a king). A negative 1 ◇ is then 0–5 and many advantages arise from this.

I have not been a candidate for international teams (apart from Camrose matches) since Estoril, and I don't suppose I shall be again. For one thing, I have become somewhat deaf and that is tiresome for everyone unless bidding boxes are used. I first played with bidding boxes in the Pairs Olympiad at Stockholm in 1970 and I have urged their adoption ever since. Players indicate their call by placing on the table a coloured card taken from a box which is arranged like an alphabetical index. No doubt about the calls made, no need to review the bidding or ask the contract, no possibility of mishearing, no verbal emphasis; it makes me sick to hear the plaint, 'We are not used to them.' Spectators are entitled to some considera-tion, too.

Tournament bridge is too young a game for any final conclusions to be drawn about the effect of age. Kenneth Konstam and Harrison-Gray were both tremendous forces in the game till the end of their lives; both were in the late sixties and neither had good health. I do not feel that my faculties have diminished, but I am not so keen or ambitious as I used to be. I have won the Masters Pairs six times and I don't think that record will be overtaken because the event is open now to all Life Masters and the list grows longer every year. The Gold Cup, however, has eluded me in recent years. I have won it eight times, but Boris has won it ten times. I shall go on trying to overtake him even when my role in good teams is restricted to that of board-carrier.

In 1975, when the European Championship was played in Brighton, I acted as chief commentator on bridgerama, ably assisted by Chris Dixon, Patrick Jourdain and Sam Leckie. During the championship I received my award as winner of the first Bols Bridge Tips competition. The essence of my tip was that declarer should watch the early discards and draw the appropriate inferences. I illustrated the advice with a hand where declarer's holding in a side suit was:

$$\heartsuit \text{ K J x x}$$

$$\heartsuit \text{ x x}$$

Eventually South has to take a guess in this suit. If East has discarded one or two hearts the odds are that he began with A x x x or similar; but if he has clung tenaciously to his original holding it is probably because he began with Q x x x and was reluctant to unguard the queen in case South held A x.

Although the Italians, when they played on bridgerama, seemed to give their opponents many chances, they were in a winning position from half way. For most of the time it looked as though France, and then Britain, would be second, but the Israelis finished with a series of maximum scores to snatch second place from Britain. The Israelis began their late run with a 20– —3 win against France. This match contained a sensational deal which surely would have won the Bols Brilliancy Prize, had this been instituted a year earlier.

North dealer
E-W vulnerable

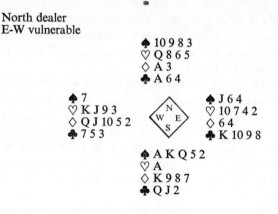

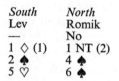

The French bid 1 ♠–3 ♠–4 ♠, as most of us would have done. Lev and Romik, playing the Roman club, reached the difficult slam.

South	North
Lev	Romik
—	No
1 ◇ (1)	1 NT (2)
2 ♠	4 ♠
5 ♡	6 ♠

(1) All opening bids of one are forcing in the system. South opens 1 ◇ because he intends to show a strong hand by bidding a higher-ranking suit on the next round.

(2) A reponse of 1 ♡ would be a negative; 1 NT was constructive.

South made a good start by winning the diamond lead in hand. Then he drew trumps, cashed ♡ A, and took the club finesse. East won and returned a club (as it turned out, a red suit would have been better). Declarer won in hand, with the remaining cards as follows:

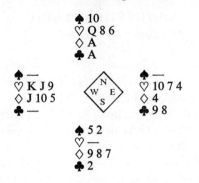

♠ 10
♡ Q 8 6
◊ A
♣ A

♠ —
♡ K J 9
◊ J 10 5
♣ —

♠ —
♡ 10 7 4
◊ 4
♣ 9 8

♠ 5 2
♡ —
◊ 9 8 7
♣ 2

Now a club to the ace, and what could West do? Israel's youngest star, Lev, had brought off a trump squeeze with extensions in two suits. All of which, I could not help remarking to my captive audience, must have caused a good deal of LEVity.

twenty

NO TURKISH DELIGHT

In 1976 the Olympiad was held in Monte Carlo. After lengthy trials the selectors nominated Flint-Rose, Priday-Rodrigue, Sheehan-Coyle. This was the team that had finished third at Brighton in 1975 and all had played with distinction in earlier championships.

Louis Tarlo, who had captained the Open team in recent years, had announced his retirement from this post and the players were asked by the selectors to say whom they would like as captain. My name was put forward as a unanimous choice and was promptly rejected by some officials of the B.B.L. No reason was given, but the word 'embarrassment' was whispered. For whom? I am not easily embarrassed, they should have known that. It was a turnaround, admittedly, since the Olympiad at Deauville, when Britain did not send a team because the World Bridge Federation had not formally accepted the Foster-Bourne report on the Buenos Aires affair, but I did not anticipate any unpleasantness. Anyway, there were some obstinate characters in the British team and eventually the objections, whatever they may have been, were overcome. The players might not have had much faith in my competence to perform some of the routine duties that fall to a non-playing captain, but in other respects I was really an obvious choice—*en rapport* with all members of the team and knowledgeable about the game.

We arrived in Monte Carlo just as Italy and the USA were finishing their match for the world championship. The Americans at last defeated an Italian team which, if not their strongest in terms of partnerships, contained Forquet, Belladonna and Garozzo. The Italians played under the shadow of a new set of accusations. At Bermuda the year before one of their pairs had been accused of using foot signals. (As screens were in use during the bidding, this was presumably the only way to exchange illicit communication.) The W.B.F. issued a judgement which seemed to say, 'We find them guilty of foot-tapping, but we don't find them guilty of cheating.' The latest wound to Italian pride was self-inflicted. A leading Italian player had produced what was alleged to be the tape-record of a telephone conversation in which a member of previous Italian teams admitted that he had used cigarette signals with his partner in a world championship match. Endless arguments followed about the authenticity of the tape, causing the affair to be known as the 'Bridge Watergate'.*

There were 45 teams in the Olympiad and every team met every other team in a short match of 16 boards. Often four matches were played in a day. It was an exciting and stimulating affair, so much so that nobody seemed to tire. Britain, with an easy draw to begin with, went into a good lead and continued to play well when the more difficult matches came along. Two days from the finish it looked as though Italy would win and Britain be second, but Brazil finished with a tremendous run, just as Israel had done at Brighton. The final scores were Brazil 654, Italy 648, Britain 646, with Poland next best on 621. The British ladies, meanwhile, finished second to Italy in their section.

These fine performances were poorly reported in the British press. The ways of news editors are hard to understand. Does the *Observer* think that people turn to each other with a wild surmise, saying 'I wonder where the new building for the European Assembly will be sited?' or 'Have you heard about the new playground in Bootle?' These are not fanciful questions. The suspenseful story about the siting of the new Assembly occupied about the same space in the *Observer* as my report from Monte Carlo would have done if it had been printed, and the tit-bit about the new playground in Bootle occurred on a previous occasion when a British win in the European Championship was not thought to be worth a line.

Newspapers are generally commercial in these times, which makes the intellectual chi-chi about chess all the stranger. The bridge community—I state this simply as a fact of life—is far more affluent than the chess community, and Britain has a higher world standing in bridge than in chess, yet chess tournaments receive a much better showing. At the same time, it may well be that the remedy lies in the hands—or rather, pens—of bridge players themselves, for there is no doubt that newspapers are highly sensitive to requests from readers. When the *Evening News* went 'tabloid', yielding its front

* A year later the matter had not been finally resolved. In 1977 the Americans had a scandal of their own when a pair withdrew from the final trials after an allegation whose exact nature was never revealed. Ironically, the captain of the team in question was John Gerber, who had been captain of the American team at Buenos Aires.

page to the amours of beauty queens, the bridge article was cut from
one a day to one a week, but in the first week of the new arrangement I was told that the daily article would be restored.

Encouraged by the success of its Bridge Tips competition, the
Bols Liqueur Company offered a Brilliancy Prize at Monte Carlo,
the cash awards going to journalists who first recounted the incident.
I put in a hand played by Irving Rose in the match against Israel.
The scores were dead level after 9 boards. This was board 10:

East dealer
Game all

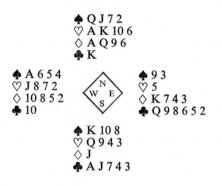

```
                    ♠ Q J 7 2
                    ♡ A K 10 6
                    ◇ A Q 9 6
                    ♣ K
    ♠ A 6 5 4                     ♠ 9 3
    ♡ J 8 7 2          N          ♡ 5
    ◇ 10 8 5 2     W       E      ◇ K 7 4 3
    ♣ 10               S          ♣ Q 9 8 6 5 2
                    ♠ K 10 8
                    ♡ Q 9 4 3
                    ◇ J
                    ♣ A J 7 4 3
```

The British pair bid as follows:

South	North
Rose	Flint
No	2 ◇ (1)
2 NT (2)	4 ◇ (3)
6 ♡ (4)	No

(1) This was the multi-coloured 2 ◇, which is usually a weak
two bid in one of the majors but may be a strong balanced hand or
a strong 3-suiter including both majors.

(2) Showing that South is willing to advance in either major,
should partner hold the weak type.

(3) Signifying the strong 3-suiter type with a shortage in clubs.

(4) 'Stand not upon the order of your going,
       'But go at once.'

It was a good hand for the system, the four bids taking about four
seconds.

With little to go on, Lev opened with ♠ A and ♠ 4, his partner playing high-low. Assuming that there is no trump loser, the declarer can count four hearts, three spades, one diamond and two clubs; so two ruffs are needed.

Many players would take two rounds of trumps early on, but Rose's play was more accurate. He won the second trick with ♠ K, crossed to ◇ A and led ◇ 6 from the table. Romik gave this a brief look, then played low. Irving ruffed, cashed ♡ Q, played ♣ 3 to ♣ K and ruffed another diamond with ♡ 9. The position was:

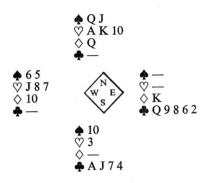

```
          ♠ Q J
          ♡ A K 10
          ◇ Q
          ♣ —
♠ 6 5                    ♠ —
♡ J 8 7                  ♡ —
◇ 10          N          ◇ K
♣ —        W   E         ♣ Q 9 8 6 2
              S
          ♠ 10
          ♡ 3
          ◇ —
          ♣ A J 7 4
```

Declarer led ♣ A and Lev did the best he could by discarding ◇ 10. Confident now that East was down to ◇ K and five clubs, Rose discarded ◇ Q and finessed ♡ 10 to land the contract. The swing was mainly responsible for Britain's win by 14 victory points to 6.

This made a good little story, I thought, but it failed to catch the judges' eye. The winner of the first prize was Ron Klinger of Australia, for a well-executed blocking play. There were three prize-winners and I must say I was amazed that this entry by Bert Dormer, describing a defence by the popular Brazilian, Gabriel Chagas, was not among them:

No Turkish Delight

North dealer
Love all

```
               ♠ Q 4
               ♡ Q 9 2
               ◇ A K J 8 4
               ♣ J 9 3
  ♠ A K 8 2                      ♠ 10 9 6 5
  ♡ K 10 7         N            ♡ A 4 3
  ◇ Q 10 7     W      E         ◇ 5 3 2
  ♣ K 10 4         S            ♣ 8 6 2
               ♠ J 7 3
               ♡ J 8 6 5
               ◇ 9 6
               ♣ A Q 7 5
```

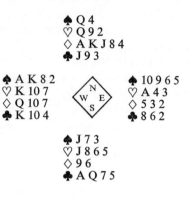

In the match between Brazil and Turkey North opened 1 ◇ and
South responded 1 NT, which was passed out. Chagas, sitting West,
opened ♠ K and his partner dropped the 10, suggesting an even
number of cards but denying the jack. Realizing that it was important to prevent South from gaining entry for the diamond finesse,
Chagas followed with ♠ 2 to dummy's ♠ Q.

South now led ♣ J from the table. Giving him a chance to go
wrong, West dropped the 10. There were chances now to make four
club tricks, so declarer followed with ♣ 9 from dummy. This,
again, was allowed to hold. Next came ♣ 3 to ♣ Q, losing to ♣ K.

This was not very bright, perhaps, on South's part. A defender
with 10 4 alone would hardly have played the 10 under the jack on
the first round, as this could easily cost a trick.

From this point on, there was no Turkish delight. West cashed
♠ A and led ♠ 8 to his partner's 9, dummy discarding a heart and a
diamond. Then came ♡ A and another; dummy was down to ♡ Q
alone, so Chagas put in the 10, forcing dummy to win and lead
away from ◇ A K J. Thus the defence came to seven tricks by way
of three spades, two hearts, one diamond and one club.

The banquet after Monte Carlo was honoured by the presence of
Prince Rainier and Princess Grace. During the cabaret Rob
Sheehan and I disgraced ourselves (a little drink goes a long way
with me) by thumping the table and shouting 'Rangers! Rangers!',
battle-cry of Q.P.R., to the intense embarrassment of the British
ladies' captain.

The organizers of the championship accomplished the enormous task of dealing all the hands in advance and duplicating them so that the same hands would be played in every match. This greatly increased the interest for players and journalists, but it also raised, or was thought to raise, a security problem. Could spectators be allowed to wander? At first only non-playing captains and official scorers were allowed into the so-called open room and even they had to stay at their own table. It thus became a non-event for spectators. In an interview for the *Bulletin* I was quoted as saying:

The tournament committees act as though they were conducting a security operation instead of presenting a sporting contest. You won't get true security, in the bridge sense, until we play in sound-proof, windowless boxes. By that time the game will be dead.

The official explanation was that the measures were necessary to protect the players from innuendo. ('What made him drop the singleton king of clubs? Somebody must have given him the wig-wags.') This is the argument for table screens, which were used in the world championship match, though not in the Olympiad. In my opinion, the last state is worse than the first. 'I felt as though I were playing with a pistol pressed against the back of my neck', one of the Italian players said to me, describing the atmosphere during the last session of the Bermuda Bowl. When these matters were dis-cussed at a meeting of the International Bridge Press Association, a speaker from New Zealand made the sound point that anything which serves to emphasize the difference between tournament play and rubber bridge is bad for the image of the game.

Two recent changes in the duplicate Laws proceed from the same kind of exaggerated suspiciousness. At the end of the auction the leader's partner is not allowed to ask for a review of the bidding, in case his questions may be thought to suggest a lead. Thus we have the inexpressibly tedious business of the leader placing his card face downwards, to allow his partner to ask a question after the lead has been selected and before dummy has been exposed.

Secondly, the system of alerting has gone crazy. At one time a player intending to make a pre-emptive bid was exhorted to say, for example, STOP—3 ♡, so that the next player, pausing for a man-datory ten seconds, could collect his thoughts and call without giving any improper information, as by a slow pass or a speedy double. There was some sense in this, but not much. Then it was found that table scorers (who were supposed to interject STOP at the appropriate moment) could not aways distinguish between a pre-empt and a strong bid, so the rule was 'simplified'. Players are now required to say STOP whenever a round of bidding is by-passed. So you get 1 NT —pass—STOP 3 NT, when obviously the player who may have a problem is the one who has to call over 1 NT, not his partner. In many cases a double, which does not raise the level of the bidding at all, can create a very awkward problem for the next player.

How little this fatuous regulation is understood by the average run of players is shown by an incident at a recent Eastbourne Congress. The player on my right opened 1 ♣ and I overcalled with an intrepid STOP—3 ♡. The lady on my left was puzzled and my partner explained that she was required to pause for ten seconds before making her call.

'Oh?' said the lady. 'Well, when my ten seconds are up, I'm going to double.'

INDEX

A.C.B.L. Bulletin, 97
Albany Club, 2
Albarran, Pierre, 18
Allinger, 101
Anne Reese Cup, 28
Anulf, 37
Avarelli, 89, 93–4

Bach, 10
Bacherich, 69, 73, 102
Barbour, Ken, 110–13
Bardola, 107
Basset Scott, 6
BBC, 28–9, 32–3, 98
Beasley, Colonel, 19
Becker, 88, 90
Belladonna, Giorgio, 59, 76, 89, 93–4, 126, 132
Bermuda Bowl, Buenos Aires, 1965, 117–18; Monte Carlo, 1976, 76–7
Bernasconi, 107–8
Besse, Jean, 69, 75–6
Bianchi, 59, 107–8
Bishop, 53, 55, 60, 65
Bludhorn, 25
Bols Liqueur Company, 129, 134
Bourchtoff, 83, 102
Le Bridge, 18
Bridge Magazine, 2–3, 6–9, 18, 43, 53–4, 60, 92, 111–12, 124
'Bridge on the Air', 28–31, 69
Bridge Player's Dictionary, 34
Bridge with Mr Playbetter, 45–51
Bridge World (U.S.A.), 97, 106 118, 122
British Bridge League (B.B.L.), 6, 7, 9–10, 27–8, 41–2, 67, 77–8, 81, 110, 114, 123, 127, 132
British Bridge World, 3, 6–7, 8–9, 11, 40, 69, 78, 88, 91–2, 96, 101, 103, 110, 112, 113
Brogi, 107–8
Brown, Sanborn, 83
Buller, Colonel Walter, 2–3, 11, 12, 19

Camrose trials, 37–8
Cansino, Jonathan, 118, 126, 127
Chagas, Gabriel, 135–6
Chiaradia, 59, 90, 97–8
Cohen, Ben, 7
Cohn, Martin, 83
Collings, 118
The Complete Book of Bridge, 34
Contract Bridge Association of Ireland, 118
Contract Bridge Journal, 37–8, 41–2, 43, 52, 69, 96
Corwen, Reg, 59, 61, 97
Cotter, 10
Country Life, 78
Coyle, 132
Crawford, Johnny, 52, 88, 90
Cremoncini, 107, 109
Crockford's, 52
Crockford's Cup, 28
Culbertson, Ely, 3, 12–18, 19, 21, 22, 24, 56, 69
Culbertson, Josephine, 3, 12–17, 18, 20, 22, 24

Daily Telegraph, 77–8, 88, 91
D'Alelio, 86, 90
De La Rue, 61, 69, 83
Delmouly, Claude, 102, 126
Develop Your Bidding Judgement, 34

Dillon, Douglas, 71
Dixon, Chris, 129
Dodds, Leslie, 10, 11, 37, 42, 43, 53, 55, 59, 71–2, 77
Domville, Sir Guy, 19
Dormer, Albert, 34, 40–1, 96, 110, 135–6
D'Unienville, 42
Duplicate Bridge Board of Control, 9–10

Edward Arnold Ltd, 34
Eisenberg, 76–7
Elements of Contract, 3
Ellenby, 53–4, 56, 60–2
English Bridge Union (E.B.U.), 9, 27–8, 113, 115
European Bridge League, 120
European Bridge Review, 38, 43
European Championship, Budapest, 1937, 10; Copenhagen, 1948, 36–7; Paris, 1949, 37; Brighton, 1950, 41–2; Venice, 1951, 41–2; Dun Laoghaire, 1952, 43–4; Helsinki, 1953, 52, 53; Montreaux, 1954, 59–60; Amsterdam, 1955, 67–9, 77; Stockholm, 1956, 74–6, 77–8; Vienna, 1957, 81–2; Oslo, 1958, 42, 91; Palermo, 1959, 97–8; Torquay, 1961, 106–9; Baden-Baden, 1963, 113–14, 117; Dublin, 1967, 118–20; Oslo, 1969, 120–2, 123–4; Estoril, 1970, 127–8; Brighton, 1975, 129
Evening News, 7, 35, 36, 133–4
The Expert Game, 34

Fagan, B. W., 34
Farrington, Frank, 40
Fell, Geoffrey, 43
Field, 6
Field, Myron, 70, 72
Filarski, Herman, 38
Fishbein, 92–3

Fisher, Sir Nigel, 4
Fleming, Mrs, 53
Flint, Jeremy, 98, 113, 117, 118, 120, 122, 126, 127, 132, 134
Forbes, Dr, 83
Forquet, 59, 76, 91, 97–8, 115, 132
Foster-Bourne report, 117, 120, 132
Four Aces, 22–3
Franco, 59–60, 77
Franklin, Harold, 29, 43, 44, 61, 75, 83, 86, 106, 124
Franks, 97
Frost, Kenneth, 20
Fry, Sam Jr., 92
Furse, Niel, 36

Gardener, Nico, 42, 53, 81, 98, 106, 109, 110, 121–2
Garozzo, Benito, 38, 77, 126, 132
Ghestem, 69–71, 73, 102
Giovine, 59–60
Glick, Jeff, 70
Gold Cup, 1937, 10–11; 1947, 36
Goldstein, 118
Gordon, 127
Gordon, Mrs, 78, 110
Goren, Charles, 65, 70, 71, 83, 85, 86, 101
Gottlieb, Mike, 17, 22–3
Griffiths, J. N. R., 114–15
Gruenther, Lt., 12, 16
Guardian, 125

Hamilton, 76
Hamilton Club, 37
Harding, Colin, 52
Harkavy, Harold, 65
Harmon, 92–4
Harrison-Gray, 2, 4, 10, 11, 24–5, 28, 37, 42–3, 69, 78, 91, 112–13, 117, 118, 128
Harrison-Gray, Stella, 35

Hasler, Alex, 35
Hazen, Lee, 70, 72, 92–3
Heidenfeld, 86
Herbert, 25
Hervey, George F., 18
Hiron, 118
Hughes, 20–1, 22

Ingram, Harry, 10, 20–1, 22–3, 40, 43, 44, 96
International Bridge League, 7, 10
International Bridge Press Association, 137
ITV, 33

Jacobi, 107
Jacoby, Oswald, 12–16
Jais, 69–70, 73, 102, 110, 113
Jannersten, Eric, 91–2, 94
Jellinek, 24–5
Johnson, Benjamin O., 54
Jourdain, Patrick, 129
Juan, Pedro, 4, 27, 78–9

Kahn, 70
Kehoe, 11
Kempson, Ewart, 10, 24, 26, 43, 60, 96, 111–12
Klinger, Ron, 135
Kock, 37, 86
Konstam, Kenneth, 10, 24–6, 37, 43, 53, 55, 59–60, 62, 64, 65, 69, 71–2, 77, 81, 97, 106, 111–13, 117, 128

Lady, 36, 45
Lampitt, L. F., 35
Lattès, 69
Lazard, 92
Lazarus, 97
Leckie, Sam, 129
Lederer, Dick, 4–5, 10, 11, 20, 22
Lederer, Peggy, 5
Lederer, Tony, 5
Lederers, 3–4, 10, 36
Leist, Hans, 52

Lenz, Sidney, 12–17
Lester, Mrs, 78
Lev, 130–1, 134–5
Leventritt, Peter, 61
Lightner, Teddy, 14, 21
Lilliehook, 37
Lock, 10
London and Home Counties Contract Bridge Association, 9, 27
Lotbinière, S. J. de, 28

McLaren, Charles, 2–3, 83
Macleod, Iain, 2, 4, 11, 41, 43, 52
Macpherson, Stewart, 28–9
Manning-Foster, A. E., 2, 6–7, 9, 28
Markus, Rixi, 57, 78, 110, 122–3
Marx, Jack, 4, 42
Mascheroni, 107, 109
Mathe, Lew, 53, 56, 60–2, 101
Mathieson, 10–11, 24–6
Maugham, W. Somerset, 69
Mayer, Edward, 55, 71
Melville Smith, Dr, 7, 35
Meredith, 'Plum', 4, 37, 42, 43, 55, 56, 57, 59–60, 62, 65, 68–9, 78, 81, 97
Merkin, Stanley, 24–6
Milford, 127
Mobbs, Sir Noel, 28, 41, 42
Mollo, Victor, 51
Moran, 60–3
Morehead, Albert, 20, 22
Morris, George, 19
Moyse, Sonny, 122

National Bridge Association, 7, 9
Newmark, Herbert, 22–3
Nexon, Baron de, 69
Norman, Stanley, 80
North, Freddie, 118, 121

Oakie, 53, 55, 56

Observer, 6, 34, 35, 80–1, 97, 133
Ogust, 101–2
Olympiad, Turin, 1960, 98–102; New York, 1964, 114–15; Deauville, 1968, 120, 132; Monte Carlo, 1976, 132–7
Ortiz-Patino, Jimmy, 71, 75, 89, 107–8

Pairs Olympiad, Cannes, 1962, 110; Stockholm, 1970, 128
Pavlides, Jordanis, 59, 63, 65
Phillips, Edmund, 40
Phillips, Hubert, 3, 7, 9, 10, 18, 35, 36, 45, 69
Play Bridge with Reese, 34
Potter, Stephen, 87
Priday, Jane, 79
Priday, Tony, 79, 106, 109, 118, 121–2, 132
Pugh, John, 118, 121, 127

Ramsey, Guy, 37–8, 41–2, 77–8, 88, 91, 98
Rapee, 88, 91
Raphael, Frederic, 117
Rayne, Eddie, 37, 42
Reese, Anne, 1–2, 4, 19
Reese, John, 1–2, 3
Reese, Max, 1–2, 34
Reese on Play, 34
Reeve, 10
Regency Club, 5
Reithoffer, 86
Riddell, Henry, 29, 69
Rockfelt, Dr, 44, 68
Rodrigue, 106, 120–1, 132
Romanet, 69
Romik, 130, 135
Root, Bill, 65
Rose, Albert, 53, 81, 83, 98, 106, 109, 117
Rose, Irving, 118, 132, 134–5
Rose, Willie, 20, 22, 53

Rosen, 53–5, 57, 60–3
Roth, Alvin, 60–1, 89, 90

Savostin, 86
Schapiro, Boris, 36–7, 38, 41, 43, 52, 55, 56, 59, 62–3, 65, 68, 71–3, 77–8, 81, 91, 97–8, 102, 110, 112–15, 117–18, 121–2, 129
Schenken, Howard, 17, 22–3, 89, 101–2
Schneider, 24–6
Schwab Cup, 1933, 19; 1934, 19–22
Seamon, Billy, 65
Selby, Harold, 27, 28
Shanahan, Dorothy, 78
Sharif, Omar, 126–7
Sharples, J., 91
Sharples, R., 91
Sheehan, Rob, 132, 136
Sheinwold, Alfred, 53–4, 69
Sherrington, Alwyn, 125–6
Silodor, 88, 90
Simmons, 11
Simon, Carmel, 35–6
Simon, S. J. ('Skid'), 4, 9, 10, 27, 35–6, 37, 42, 51
Siniscalco, 91
Slavenburg, Bobby, 120
Sobel, Helen, 83, 85
Solomon, 70, 72
Squire, Norman, 59, 83, 96
Stakgold, 92–4
Stanley, 118
Star, 2
Stayman, Sam, 70, 72
Steen, 53
Stern, Dr Paul, 24, 25–6
Stone, 89, 90
Story of an Accusation, 117
Summers, 11
Sunday Times, The, 113, 126
Svarc, 83
Swimer, 98, 118, 122–3
Swinnerton-Dyer, Peter, 53, 110–13

Tabbush, Percy, 19
Tait, Jimmy, 113–14
Tarlo, Bea, 44
Tarlo, Joel, 42, 67–9, 97, 111, 113
Tarlo, Louis, 42, 43, 44, 59, 75, 98, 120–1, 132
Telfer, Colonel Roy, 104
Thorne, Harold, 19
Thorneley, H. L., 7–8
Times, The, 6
Tottenham, 10
Tournament Bridge Association (T.B.A.), 27–8, 41
Traub, Alec, 104
Trewin, J. C., 35
Trézel, 69–70, 73, 102, 110, 113
Truscott, Alan, 42, 69, 72, 78, 91, 106, 109
Tuite, Hugh, 51

Van Rees, Marjorie, 78

Von Zedtwitz, 65

Waddington Cup for Masters Pairs, 28
Walshe, Colonel, 20
Weissberger, Maurice, 125
Werner, 37
Westall, Bernard, 7
Williams, Mrs, 78
Winfield Liggett, Commander, 16–17
Withers, Mollie, 36
Wohlin, 37
Work, Milton, 2
World Bridge Federation, 120, 132
World Championship, New York, 1955, 60–5; Paris, 1956, 69–71; New York, 1959, 91–5

Yallouze, 86, 126